to Hannah
Best wishes ~
Christine
X

MEMOIRS of LONDON

From 1960's to Present Day

By
Christine Levy

Edited by
Joshua Ben Levy

Strategic Book Group

Strategic Book Group
P.O. Box 333
Durham CT 06422
www.StrategicBookClub.com

ISBN 978-1-60911-751-1

This book is dedicated to my children.

Table of Contents

Who Am I?

I have memories of exploring isolated cliffs and sandbanks as a child on the cold North East coast of Yorkshire, a working class home life which at times seemed quite deprived but nearly always entertaining, in a village which felt like being surrounded by a larger extended family who were financially also on a very low income.

I remember Brownies, Girl Guides and then 'Bopping' (jive) in luminous green bobby socks and black drainpipe trousers to Bill Haley & the Comets in the local, Marske-by-sea, near Tees-side youth club, Tommy Steele, Cliff Richards and Buddy Holly burst onto the 1950's teenage scene and this was a time when many parents felt that their children had 'taken over.'

Outgrowing village life early I found a job in Leeds and felt part of a big city where my 'going out on the town' days really began. After two years there I travelled abroad a lot, visiting remote places which was an out of the norm thing to do in those days. When my travelling escapades came to an end I finished up in London.

In the first year, I found myself constantly changing addresses until I finally came to a decision to emigrate to Canada with some like minded travellers. However, fate stepped in and I met Ariel Levy in the Roebuck pub on Pond Street, opposite the Royal Free Hospital in Hampstead and he was from Camden Town. I eventually got married to him whilst taking up permanent residency in North West London.

We had three children: They were Sophie, who was born in 1968, Joshua in 1971 and lastly Charlotte in 1979, which was just prior to Ariel getting itchy feet and heading off to Los Angeles with his new Californian partner.

Outside of this personal life-changing event, I believe many people in this area and beyond can relate to what I have written as the experiences span decades and cover the various phases of lifestyle, fashion, music etc, commonly depicted in general and personal terms.

The flash of inspiration for this book came to me as I was walking one time on Hampstead Heath.

MEMOIRS of LONDON
From 1960's to Present Day

Chapter One

LONDON IN THE SWINGING 60's

The music of the 1950's encouraged an identity and opened up a whole new world to young people, which set the scene for the coming 60's. The fashions suddenly became outrageous, with skinny models in tight mini-skirts and very obviously made-up faces. Pale shades of cream covered the face and black eyeliner round the whole eyes; inevitably grabbing attention and depicting the times. Top fashion model, Twiggy, looking thin, pale, gauche and young, was discovered, by the then leading photographer, David Bailey. Her looks summed up an era that many girls consequently copied.

London was the fashion capital of the world and Carnaby Street in the West End became the focal point for clothes shopping and for every fashion-stating social scene. Designer, Mary Quant opened the first boutique, which was 'Bazaar' in Chelsea. She was known for her outlandish designs, mini skirts and for the famous 'Vidal Sassoon' haircut. Her designs were both fun, yet inexpensive.

Towards the end of the sixties one of the trends we had was the birth of the hippy cult and 'Flower Power!' The famous slogan 'Make Love Not War' arrived, which was synonymous with free sex and the American anti-war movement against the Vietnam War. There was an anti-war demo at the American Embassy with an 80,000 strong crowd and famous actress/peace campaigner, Vanessa Redgrave, spoke out at this rally. Paint and stones were also hurled at the American Embassy as well. Also the largest Ban the Bomb demonstration took place in Trafalgar Square with more than 15,000 protesters taking part and 850 people got arrested for causing chaos. On that march, Nobel Prize winner Bertrand Russell and playwright Arnold Wesker were jailed for inciting a breach of the peace.

There were 'beautiful' people all over London who would often be seen walking over Hampstead Heath and through the streets – shoeless. Illustrating some of this was the hippy musical 'Hair' that first appeared on stage at the Roundhouse in Chalk Farm. The show was a deafening 'tribal-love-rock' musical and its use of four-letter words shocked London and most of Britain at that time and the naked performers at the end of the show caused great consternation and wonderment because this was the first occurrence of 'baring all' in a London staged musical.

Acid (LSD,) magic mushrooms and cannabis became an integral part of hippiedom life, and other aspects of the hippy lifestyle appeared such as Eastern methods of relaxation and inner searching. The Beatles exemplified this when they went to see the Maharishi yogi, to look for inner peace and an end to all drug taking. However, marijuana-mania swept out of control on the streets; 'Cannabis, pot, charge, bush, grass, hash, dope, reefers, joints, spliffs, etc,' were just some of the alternative names used to describe this drug. "Britain's Youth Go Potty!" screamed the tabloids.

Joining in the trend, some friends I knew from Hawaii came to visit London with pockets full of weed. They explained to us that getting incredibly stoned had become for them a way of life and was certainly something we should try for ourselves. We joined them in the fun of the moment and feeling rather high, left together to go to a local party. We arrived at the party but I could not speak to our hosts because I was completely 'spaced out' and I found that acutely embarrassing.

In those days, I began working as a mathematical typist and secretary for the computer wizards who set up Logica and commuting to my office job in the West End started with getting on the tube at Belsize Park which is between Camden and Hampstead in North-West London. Around that time many people were reading 'Lady Chatterley's Lover' by D.H. Lawrence and due to the controversy surrounding this book, I saw the readers concealing their copies with brown paper covers. The Director of Public Prosecutions took the publishers 'Penguin' to court under the Obscene

Publications Act at the Old Bailey in London, from 20th October to 2nd November 1960 because the book describes a torrid love affair between the Lady of the Manor and her Gamekeeper. The book was laced with four letter words but was eventually declared 'not obscene' by an Old Bailey jury!

In this decade, Harold Wilson became the first Labour Prime Minister since Clement Atlee, some twenty years earlier.

Fay Weldon's phrase 'Go to work on an egg!' came to her when she was working on an advert for the British Egg Marketing Board and this opened the door to fame and notoriety as a writer. Fay and her husband Ron owned an antique shop in Primrose Hill and were close friends of ours on the North London scene. Many memories of dinners and parties were shared and even today I still have furniture that I bought from Ron at ridiculously low prices.

The first ever push-button controlled 'zebra' crossings were introduced.

Sean Connery made his screen debut as '007 James Bond.' It was the first film and book in the Ian Fleming series and was emphatically named 'Dr. No.'

Mrs. Mary Whitehouse became famous for her 'Clean up TV' campaign and was combating what she saw as immorality on television. Most people will remember television in those days as far milder. However we had Alf Garnett on TV portraying an 'Old East Ender' who behaved like a prejudicial bigot and hated changes in Society. He had a quick mind and picked up on people's frailties and we thought at the time that he was hilarious with his 'no holds barred speech,' something that would probably be banned nowadays.

Enoch Powell, M.P., received attention with his anti-immigration speeches, expressing famous phrases such as "Rivers of Blood" and called Britain "the sick man of Europe!" He stated that allowing an inflow of dependants of immigrants into this country each year is like watching a nation "busily engaged in heaping up its own funeral pyre" and that "in this country in fifteen or twenty years time, the black man will have the whip hand over the white man."

His speech was said to be racialist in tone and was compared with the attitudes of Nazi Germany. He was dismissed from the Shadow Cabinet by Ted Heath, PM, which many said was an attack on the British right of free speech. (For quotes, search 'enochpowell.net')

England won football's World Cup in 1966 against Germany and the result was a clear 4-2 victory! Both teams played the final at Wembley Stadium on Saturday July 30th. England led 2-1 until the end of the game when the match went into extra time, where they finally won 4-2. The game was said to be the height of English sporting achievement; well it certainly was for football, even to this day.

Gangland twins Ronald and Reginald Kray who were said to have terrorized the 'east end' were given life sentences for murder. They were arrested on May 9th 1968 and convicted in 1969 of the murders of Jack 'the hat' McVitie and George Cornell. Prior to this in 1960 I was working as a chambermaid in hotels on the Isle of Jersey and was acquainted with a young man whose father owned a pub in the East End which the Krays frequented. He told me that the twins were coming over to Jersey for a holiday which resulted in my being introduced to this infamous pair one afternoon whilst sunbathing on the beach in St. Brelades Bay. Although at the time I hardly believed their notoriety for crime and violence but what I did notice was that they exuded a very dark energy behind their dark glasses and tailor made suits and despite the suaveness of these men, I had no interest to know them further. (For further information search 'Kraytwins murder trial'.)

One Saturday night, some of the East End mob broke into the garage below the flat which I shared with four other girls in St. Helier and took off with the safe from the wall. When the CID came round the next day, they saw a photograph on the mantelpiece of my friend sitting between the Kray Twins on the beach, but we remembered our prior warning by the Mob, "not to mention who we knew on the Island!"

London said "Goodnight All!" (Sergeant Dixon's famous phrase) after 21 years of Jack Warner, who played this avuncular character under the Police station blue lamp. He would fight the villains of Dock Green, in the East End, hence the series being named 'Dixon of Dock Green.'

Damage estimated at £15,000 was caused when Scottish fans tore up the pitch at Wembley Stadium, after Scotland beat England 2-1.

The Murder Bill (Abolition of the Death Penalty) and Race Relations Bill became law.

A '70mph' speed limit on motorways was introduced but before then, one could drive at any speed.

The 'Profumo scandal' brought Christine Keeler and Mandy-Rice Davies into the spotlight. John Profumo, the Secretary of State for War, met call-girl Christine Keeler on Lord Astor's Clivedon estate, whilst she was frolicking naked in the swimming pool. Osteopath and artist Dr. Stephen Ward was seen as the ring master of the nation's security sex circus. He was the link between high society and low life and consequentially connected people together. Keeler had sex with Soviet agent Eugene Ivanov, among others and the scandal rocked Britain when it became clear that our national security was at stake. Ward arranged parties at his London flat and Clivedon cottage, where attractive young call girls like Christine Keeler and Mandy Rice-Davies would meet important and influential men (even notorious slum landlord Peter Rachman.) Ward was found guilty of living off immoral earnings and he died from a drug overdose on the final day of his trial. There were also rumours that he was on MI5's pay roll.

The Beatles recorded at EMI studios in St. John's Wood, which is somewhat revealed on the front cover of their aptly named 'Abbey Road' album.

'Beatlemania' had gripped the nation with their music and attributable 'mop top' hairstyles. Their No. 1s would sometimes be in the charts for months on end and teenagers rioted wherever they went, especially the occasion when they received their MBE at Buckingham Palace. The investiture looked like the storming of the Bastille with hundreds of fans outside the gates acting like a mob trying their best to get in.

In 1963, I was taken to see the Beatles perform at the 'Hammersmith Odeon' and the girls near the front of the stage were intermittently carried off as they were overcome with fainting fits of hysteria. It was not only a unique experience for me but the world had never seen or heard any band play music like that before. I realise now how incredibly fortunate I was to participate in that (particular event) when it had reached its most raw and revolutionary peak.

When I saw 'The Who' make their first appearance on stage at the 'Hippodrome' in Leicester Square, I felt immediately after seeing them perform that they would also become famous. When they played round the corner at the 'Marquee' on Charing Cross Road, they defiantly smashed up their instruments on stage. The band's music developed a 'Mod following,' who rode around on Lambrettas and Vespa scooters with their definitive Parka jackets, Dr. Marten boots, sta-pressed trousers and short styled hair;

a stark contrast to their 'Rocker' rivalling counterpart, who rode Triumph motorbikes and had a rougher, more rugged look with their definitive leather jackets, biker boots, turned-up jeans and gelled, rockabilly styled hair and they loved to dance to the rock'n'roll music from the 1950's.

There were the infamous riotous clashes at Brighton beach on Bank Holiday Mondays and through the Sunday papers the general public were advised to 'lock up their daughters!'

Then came the 'Rolling Stones,' who defied style completely and had a new founded hippy following. Unlike the Beatles' pop sounding music, the Rolling Stones introduced for the first time a more 'Rock' based sound.

Police seized Andy Warhol's film 'Flesh' from the Open Space theatre in 1968 because of its sexually graphic footage.

In 1969, from minority taste to cult status, the 'Monty Python's Flying Circus' became TV's nearest equivalent to radio four's 'Goon Show' and their humour was quintessentially English.

LONDON IN THE 60's
(A MORE PERSONAL ACCOUNT)

Unusual Sights

In the early 60's I went to 'Biba,' a famous dress shop in South Kensington which was known to be the trendiest fashion place in London for young people. After a visit there, I got on the 60's youth bandwagon and purchased the shortest skirt I've ever worn which just covered my knickers.

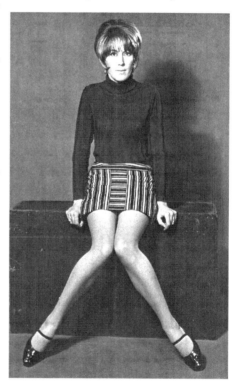

Feeling very hip, I stepped out of my maisonette on St. John's Wood High Street and an old man who was passing saw me in this state of undress and not believing his eyes, dropped his jaw, shopping bag and walking stick. However, I did not go to his assistance as that would have meant bending down and I still had to learn the art of manoeuvring without appearing indecent. The mini-skirt took a while to catch on as a fashion item and at first only the young would dare to be so sparsely clad but within a couple of years most females, including older women wore short skirts, so no doubt as time went on, the old man would have grown accustomed to seeing many mini-clad females.

Driving Test

Perhaps the mini-skirt helped me because I passed the driving test first time. My first car was an old style black London cab, which nowadays would be unlikely to sell at £80. It was easy to drive but the first time I took it for a spin I drove out too eagerly and watching me leave at the side of the road, I unfortunately ran over my friend's foot.

When Sophie, my eldest daughter was born, I found it wonderful to put the whole pram with her in the back, as well as friends, who really enjoyed not having to pay the fare. It took around three months to drive well and people, mistaking my car for a real London cab, would frequently step off the curb to hail me down. One time, whilst driving through the West End, a real working cab driver passed me and shouted "get out of my way; you'll never make a cab driver!"

Incredible Laughter

A couple of close friends were Hetta and Josh from Hampstead. We would drive down to the remote countryside of Suffolk, not in my trusty cab but in their car, which happened to be an old ambulance. On our journey we would play cards and drink wine in the back and there was always a chamber pot for emergencies. Our final destination was 'Hares Creek' and a remote cottage overlooking the Orwell River.

We would take off through London and out onto the A12 towards Ipswich on what seemed to be an endlessly straight road. Just before Ipswich we would turn right onto minor roads towards Shotley, through Chelmondiston and a bit further before turning left and then finally bumping our way down a long earthy track, pitted and narrow, all the way to the cottage. Once inside we would light the oil lamp and the small fire which heated the oven so we could have tea and toast. Cleaning wasn't on the agenda and so among the debris and bits of old candlewax we would find a spot for the bottles of wine. At first on spending time with Hetta I felt quite in awe of her natural power and charisma. Her tall statuesque South African figure and beauty invariably attracted attention. Also, her powerful presence and together with her boyfriend Josh, who was much younger and had film star looks, made them both a striking and riveting pair.

We would walk beside the Orwell River to an old pub called the 'Butt & Oyster' where once inside surrounded by dark oak panels, we would begin to feel warm and inebriated.

The cottage was quite primitive with thankfully no attempt at modernisation and not even the spiders' webs were ever removed. We spent many weekends being very jolly and enjoyed collecting mussels and sea asparagus from the river bed, plus blackberries from the many surrounding tangled bushes, for our delicious evening feasts. Cooking on the open fire was an art to be mastered and required a great amount of patience as it always took so much longer than a normal stove. Outside of the kitchen door in a shed was the 'privvy' or 'loo' which was a fairly large box with a seat, in which to do your no.2s. We called this 'the latrine,' the contents of which had to be buried before returning to London.

Back in London

We would frequent the many curry houses in Hampstead and next door's South End Green, whilst continuously drinking and inevitably talking loudly. After a few glasses of red we all assumed we were world authorities on any given subject and after a while looking around, we saw the restaurant had become unnoticeably empty. Maybe it was a coincidence but on reflection we presumed we were the cause of driving everyone out. Sometimes the night would be rounded off with falling asleep in the late night cinema on Haverstock Hill, again just down the hill from Hampstead. On one occasion, I remember struggling to stay awake to see an old black and white Italian film called 'La Strada' starring Antony Quinn and hearing snores from Hetta, Josh and Ariel. I also eventually succumbed to the wine and the warmth of the cinema and unintentionally joined them. Heads dropping forward and back, the four of us being oblivious to the fact that the film was even being played.

Celebration

Our friend Hetta's husband William was knighted for his contribution to English literature and poetry. To celebrate Sir William and Lady Hetta Empson had a crowded party in their home, which was called Studio House, on the corner of Rosslyn Hill and Hampstead Hill Gardens, NW3. Most of the then Hampstead fraternity turned up in all their many guises and it always amazed me to observe how many different types of people Hetta had as friends. The dancing, the music and the entire character-filled party lasted beyond the dawn.

People who knew the Empson family in those days were discreet about the open marriage between Lady Hetta and Sir William and their bizarre bohemian lifestyle. However, in November 2006, John Haffenden revealed all in his biography of these colourful and interesting beings and entitled it 'William Empson, Volume ll, Against the Christians!'

Personal Boons

I was living in St. John's Wood High Street NW8, in a maisonette above a shop and was then married to Ariel Levy who was involved in the film industry. As an Assistant Director he was working on a film at 'Pinewood Studios' called 'The Countess from Hong Kong,' directed by 'Charlie Chaplin' and starring 'Marlon Brando' and 'Sophia Loren.' One morning, Pinewood Studios phoned me to say that Charlie Chaplin's personal chauffeur-driven car would be coming to pick me up, to take me to watch the filming. The liveried chauffeur opened the door of the limo and I, dressed in 'Mary Quant' style, felt very grand and privileged stepping in, as what was the beginning part of an expectant glamorous day.

As well as meeting these famous celebrities, I got to see behind the camera scenes and on one occasion I saw Marlon Brando show disdain at Charlie Chaplin's attempt to tell him, 'a star' on how to act. Sophia Loren looked flawless in her appearance and overall it was understandably a most interesting and enjoyable occasion.

At home later, I was asked to phone Marlon Brando at his hotel to give him his call to go into the studio. Trembling when I made the telephone call, I heard a deep dulcet voice saying "Marlon here!" Moments like that I'll never forget and uncannily enough, my daughter Sophie spoke to him on the phone for about 40 minutes in Los Angeles, some 30 years later.

Arty Farty

1968: I was pregnant with daughter Sophie; I wore mini skirts and worked as a secretary for a New York art dealer in Bond Street in the West End. I met many artists and people connected with the art world through this job and I also went to the open nights of exhibitions but felt sorry for the many young, hopeful, sometimes long-haired and bearded artists who came in with their abstract paintings to show my boss. He asked them if they could paint a country scene of perhaps a lake with boats, designated for the American market, but their lack of education only allowed them to go as far as dots and dashes across the canvas. As a result my boss phoned up the colleges and complained that after three years their students were unable to earn a living.

I would trot between art galleries delivering and collecting pictures and on one of these jaunts down Bond Street to the Richard Green gallery I met 'Brien Sewell,' the famous art critic, in his then early career days. I would also shop for the boss's wife at exclusive places such as 'Burlington Arcade,' 'Fortnum and Masons' and 'Liberties.' The money was sadly not mine but nevertheless I felt wonderfully extravagant.

Around and About Hampstead in the 60's

Walking around on a summer evening you could peer through the curtainless windows of people's kitchens and living rooms: one saw mainly pine-clad rooms, sometimes revealing animated and lively dinner parties.

Dinner parties and parties were a common feature of the 60's scene in many parts of 'North West London.' We would dress up, often in Laura Ashley dresses or homemade clothes made from material of 'William Morris' design. Friends and neighbours would host enormous gatherings and you could hear pop music bellowing out of open home windows as you walked down the dimly lit streets at night.

Highgate Cemetery

When my eldest daughter was born, I proudly pushed her in the pram up Swain's Lane and into the gothic-styled Highgate Cemetery for a walk, and in 1968 the gates were permanently left open to the public without any suspecting fears. I loved the ancientness of it: gravestones with countless overgrown, twisted ivy and creepers that clasped to the names of those buried, often for one or two hundred years or sometimes more. Some of the coffins in the Sepulchre had, without a lie, skulls and hair showing (they have since been removed.) It was late in autumn and I was picking black-berries which had become supernaturally large and succulent, maybe because of all those dead bodies. It was predictably and commonly misty and getting late. I was alone but surprisingly feeling very happy and peaceful when I heard a crunching of feet on the sonorous gravel. I looked up to see a cloaked figure bearing down on me, with a deathly white face! 'Count Dracula!' I thought, whence I remembered that Bram Stoker had conjured up the idea of Dracula in this very same spooky and eerie cemetery. Scared?

A most definite yes! In fact I could feel my heart pounding when the figure came nearer and as he did, I noticed a white dog collar round his neck. Calming down and with great relief I found myself saying "Hello," to the local Vicar.

Chapter Two

LONDON IN THE 1970's

I remember my cheese cloth skirt and Afro Frizz being replaced by more 'Glam Rock' styles throughout the 70's. 'Marc Bolan' the Rock Singer moved from being Mod to Hippy and then to Glam with considerable ease, as indeed did so many others. The fashions were continually changing quickly and very dramatically.

The 'Post Office Tower' was opened on 8th October 1965 by the then Prime Minister (Harold Wilson) and at 620ft standing, was the tallest building in Britain. My friends and I went to the top and looked out over London as we slowly circled our way round in the continuously rotating restaurant. However the peace of the area known as Fitzrovia was shattered on October 31st 1971 when a bomb went off in the Post Office Tower. Although nobody made claim to the bomb attack, some people speculated that it was attributed to the anarchist group, known as the 'Angry Brigade' or the more renowned 'IRA.' The Angry Brigade was a mixture of 'Bader Meinhof's Red Army Faction' from Germany and the 'Red Brigades of Italy.'

The summer of 1976 was the hottest on record and London had temperatures of up to 950F 350C.

Also in the year 1976 along came punk and the lyrically and musically controversial group, 'The Sex Pistols,' went to No. 1 in the charts with their mock punk rock rendition of 'God Save the Queen!' This was the only No.1 slot to be disallowed any showing time on national television. The 'punks' had elaborate hairstyles with tufts of multi-coloured hair and cockerel-crest Mohicans being part of what would otherwise be a completely shaven head. They also wore safety pins in their ears, eyebrows and nostrils and wore grubby vests, ripped jeans and the proverbial sign of the times – Dr. Marten boots 'of course!' A 'God Save the Queen' record was sold in 2006 on e-bay for £12,000, and I can imagine some of those then  reckless punks wishing they had been a bit more clearheaded and conservative minded with their records, but what can you do with a head full of glue!

Londoners celebrated the Queen's Silver Jubilee in 1977 with street parties, banners, music, food and a great feeling of community, as did the punk-rock group 'The Sex Pistols' outside Buckingham Palace but not with the same honourable feeling.

The Sex Pistols also caused outrage due to their colourful language in the famous 'Bill Grundy' interview. Nobody had ever heard such use of filthy words on a mid-afternoon television programme before.

The BBC was again inundated with complaints after a boy used a four-letter word on 'Woman's Hour!'….. 'Outrageous!'

The 'Skinhead' craze was resurrected for the second time after it arose in 1969 but with a harder, more aggressive look. London was filled with shaven heads, upturned stain-washed jeans, hanging down braces, flight jackets, Crombies, Doctor Marten's 'bovver' boots and finished off with, for many, the essential cropped haircut. They would roam in gangs looking for 'aggro!' They 'gay bashed,' 'Paki bashed,' and went in large gangs to football matches.

The skins were fundamentally patriotic and some wore Union Jack T-shirts but many also said they were not members of the National Front. Alcohol and occasional glue-sniffing took the place of hippy-taking drugs amongst Punks and Skins. This fashion was not altogether negative and many Ska bands (a mix of rock and reggae) were formed.

However '2 Tone' (invented by Jerry Dammers, the keyboardist of the group 'The Specials') was a combination of Ska and the recently invented Punk music. Other 2 Tone bands invaded the scene such as the 'Beat,' 'Selecter,' 'Bad Manners' and of course North London's 'Nutty boys' who became known as 'Madness' and whose members went to the local schools and lived in the surrounding streets near us.

If you happened to walk past the local 'William Ellis School' on Highgate Road, NW5 which happened to be at the end of our 'Croftdown Road' at lunchtimes and when the school had finished for the day, it would be like witnessing a fashion parade because of all the various styles standing side by side outside the school gates. There were 'Teddy Boys' with their 'winkle picker' shoes, 'Edwardian style coats' and their essential rock 'n' roll gelled hair at the sides, with a quiff at the front. Then a few yards away were some 2nd time around Mods and Rude Boys who wore two-tone suits, sometimes with an identifiable thin black tie and some rude-boys could easily be spotted with the then famous pork pie hat. You also had punks who were again easily identifiable as a group and the members of that group did their best to look different, sporting different uses of hair colour and rips that

could occur anywhere in their black drainpipe jeans, army trousers, or in their prolific graffiti'd denim jackets, as well as the hard wearing black leather studded jackets which would some-times have the famous anarchy symbol and the names of whatever punk bands the individual happened to admire. Also standing close by were working class kids, known as skinheads, who would wear their bovver outfits, often steel capped Dr. Marten boots, drainpipe jeans with hanging-down braces (usually red,) Fred Perry T-shirts and V-necked sweaters or Ben Sherman shirts, and depending on the weather would either wear a Levi's denim jacket or a black Crombie coat when it was cold, with a carefully placed handkerchief protruding from the single outside pocket. They would look quite menacing as they stood huddled together with their close defining crop that would have resulted from the hair clipper being on either nos. 2, 1 or 0. These sub cultural groups appeared in their individualism for that relatively short phase in time.

'Finsbury Park' where Johnny Rotten, lead singer of the Sex Pistols was from and where the 'George Robey pub' was opposite what used to be called the 'Rainbow Theatre' (a prestigious North London venue for top bands in its heyday.) The Robey would host 'Ska festivals' where numerous bands would be playing all day and all of the night. On entering the venue you would see all the '2 Tone' and 'Skinhead regalia' crammed from wall to wall. Hundreds would be frantically jumping and pushing each other all over the place. If you wanted to avoid this physical 'shirts off' mayhem you could find an area at the back where you would be safe and take in the view of the skinheads with their mountain size looking bare backs, sometimes with no neck but a trusty short cropped head at the top.

In the midst of all this dynamic and unique activity, the bands would be catering for the highly charged, furious paced beat music for the somewhat insane looking audience and being something of an older fish out of water, I would make a hasty exit before the 'end of the night going home crush!'

Like the Adventure Playground on Parliament Hill Fields, where children could challenge themselves physically on the swing ropes and high wooden apparatus for climbing, which has now all been banned, due to the new health and safety laws, the George Robey venue is no more and hence sadly those uniquely stylish and powerfully atmospheric days were for that specific time only and there will forever remain.

At the 'Notting Hill Carnival' the Steel band sound came from Trinidad and Tobago, playing their traditional calypso and then as time went on they included classical, jazz, R&B and pop. By the early 70's the carnival began to show this display with the bands on floats and traditional dress to tour the streets and the All Saints Road which attracted people from the Caribbean islands. Over the years this three day spectacular grew and grew and is now a huge event with many bands of different types playing their music, usually aboard floats which go round the many streets of Notting

Hill. Violence, muggings and looting began to creep in which marred this very popular annual event for Londoners.

Clashes with the National Front occurred in Brick Lane in the East End and 300 were arrested at an anti-Nazi rally in Southall.

Karl Marx's grave in Highgate cemetery was daubed with Swastikas and evidence was shown that an attempt had been made to blow it up.

Enoch Powell predicted an 'explosion' unless there was a massive repatriation scheme for immigrants.

IRA bombing was rampant in the 70's and at times we heard distant explosions. I once had to flee from a shoe shop in Oxford Street wearing only one shoe and holding onto the other, as shoppers and staff were told to evacuate the building immediately because of a 'bomb scare!'

James Callaghan became the Labour Prime Minister after Harold Wilsons's resignation.

Missiles were thrown at the stage during the Miss World contest because of the ever increasing 'feminist' movement. The 'Gay Liberation Front' also held its first demonstration in London to protest against prejudice to homosexuals.

We had ladies in hot pants and knee high boots towards the end of the 70's decade, signifying the 'disco' scene, as did the ever famous film 'Saturday Night Fever.'

'John Conteh' became European Light Heavyweight Boxing Champion after beating German born Rudiger Schmidtge. He also beat Chris Finnegan after 15 gruelling rounds at Wembley to become British Champion, all by the tender age of 22. He lived as a neighbour of ours in Croftdown Road, NW5 and could be seen training on Parliament Hill Fields in the early mornings and would often stop by our house to chat and have a cup of tea.

'Dutch elm disease' killed so many trees in England and on Hampstead Heath that it changed forever the familiar sky-line.

The minimum fare on the Underground rose 50% to one shilling by the end of 1970.

The 'Vermeer painting' called the 'Guitar Player,' at Kenwood House on Hampstead Heath was stolen in the days when security was lax and trust was far more abounding. It was worth one million pounds and was somehow recovered. There were many theories as to how this painting was retrieved, to once more grace the Kenwood House walls. One of these theories was that a Spiritual Medium helped police trace the rolled up painting but it is still a mystery as to where and when the painting was found.

'Margaret Thatcher' brought the Tories to power in 1979 and she also became the nation's first woman Prime Minister. Her famous words were heard on the steps of 10 Downing Street: "Where there is discord, may we bring harmony, where there is despair, may we bring hope!" Words and deeds are sometimes two very different things!

The 'Roundhouse Theatre' on Chalk Farm Road was a prestigious venue for bands such as 'Pink Floyd, Hawkwind, Soft Machine, Jimi Hendrix and Marc Bolan (both now dead,) The Move, Cream, the Rolling Stones, the Doors, the Clash, Buzzcocks, Squeeze, Adam Ant, Love, Deep Purple, Kiss, Motorhead and AC/DC' to name but a few.

Another popular North London music venue was the 'Rainbow Theatre' in Finsbury Park, where 'David Bowie, Bob Marley and the Wailers, Roxy Music, Thin Lizzy, Jeff Beck, Pink Floyd, Stevie Wonder, Miles Davis, Dire Straits, Jethro Tull, Eric Clapton, Black Sabbath, Van Morrison, Queen, The Kinks, The Who, Elton John' and many more performed their music.

LONDON IN THE 70's
(A MORE PERSONAL ACCOUNT)

Vanity

In the early 70's 'Leonard,' the number one hairdresser, had every famous name go through his expert and creative fingers. His best friend Michael who was a film assistant to my husband Ariel arranged for me to visit Leonard. I felt very honoured and was at the time wearing an 'Afro Frizz,' which haloed my head and looked quite wild and hippyish and I feel represented the 70's.

"Why did you leave it to grow so long?" asked Leonard. He said nothing more but quickly took his scissors and eagerly set to work. He was creating people in the mode of the 'Shrimp' and 'Twiggy' and the 'debutante look' (very short above the ears and half fringe down one side.) Within minutes I was imitating this look. Nonplussed, I thanked the genius and set off home.

I walked from his salon in Mayfair and my head looked the size of a pea when I saw my reflection in a shop window and I then thought 'I've got to get a taxi and escape!' A taxi-driver made an excuse that he was diabetic and could not drive because he had to eat his sandwich (nobody ever wanted to come to NW5, as in those days it was like living in the sticks.) I then burst into tears and said I did not believe him and so I kept on walking again whilst calculating how long it would take for my hair to grow back to how I liked it.

Good Memories

The atmosphere in London in the 70's gave one a feeling of optimism. There was a real feeling of anticipation in the air which was almost palpable. I would rush around in the morning as a young mum, finishing my chores and then I would go off pushing my son Joshua in his pushchair over 'Parliament Hill Fields' at the bottom end of Hampstead Heath, to attend his 1 o'clock club. Then in later years he attended the Adventure Playground which was on the other side of the fence.

One day it was blowing hard, freezing and raining and upon entering the

1 o'clock club, I noticed he had slipped into the local cockney vernacular – "cor, it's blimey outside!" Also on the way, I would watch the young skinhead youths, hunched in their Crombie coats, marching side by side in their Dr. Marten boots across the misty, dew ridden fields. The skins would always spend the afternoons in the communal hut which was in the adventure playground, playing ping pong and listening to Ska music. Josh was fascinated by this trend and to this day still loves Ska. He once came home covered in mud from head to toe when some rough lads threw him into the centre of the circle-shaped rope swing. Though upset at the time, he remembers with affection so many of those local characters who are now with families of their own.

Josh at the age of 8 in 1979 used to walk himself over to the Adventure Playground. At the time the Skinheads rated 'the Adventure' as it was known and Skinhead Reggae would be blaring from the playground's hut. Before the health and safety regulations were put into action by the Government, places like the Adventure Playground were incredibly visually captivating with the wooden construction for climbing, rope apparatus and the huge wooden boat swing filled with local children and like so many things of those times, have and sadly never will be seen again.

Absorbed

At the nursery, Josh finished all the jigsaws, read all the books and played all the games. "Isn't he quiet and focused," said one of the teachers. Once finished, he then terrorised the children outside with his energy and would ride round and round the hut on his tricycle at top speed. One of the teachers did their level best to discipline Josh by sending him to the corner of the room but ended up like others, laughing at his cheeky face.

Pessimistic Circumstance

"Is this No. 12 Croftdown Road?" said an old tramp standing at my door, which used to be always open. Those were the days! "Sorry, this is no. 25!" Two weeks later, it was the same tramp with the same question. I should have taken precautions and kept the door closed but I didn't because the children wanted to run between the neighbour's houses. The next time the tramp turned up, my handbag disappeared and my bank account was then fiddled. The bank thought I was bluffing about the theft, as a woman had used my credit card to buy children's clothes in Muswell Hill. Apparently she had red hair and the bank thought it was me! Cheek! Three months later I was still inconveniently missing items from my handbag and since then I prefer not to own a handbag and also to keep my front door regretfully shut.

Optimistic Circumstance

An Irishman in Camden High Street held up a whole bus queue when he saw that I was enormously pregnant. "Can't you see the condition this woman is in?" he shouted, as he held out his burly arms to hold everyone back in order to let me on first.

Tasty

The 'French Onion man' was a local celebrity and always cycled down Croftdown Road twice a year which meant we all got to know him en route. The onions and garlic were delicious and we grew to love his welcoming and cheery face. One summer, he gesticulated wildly when he saw I was pregnant and showing the same proportions of pregnancy as did my neighbours, Elaine and Anita, who coincidentally lived a few doors up on the same side of the street.

He put it all down to "the moon!"

Splitting Up

Towards the end of the 70's there were many partners and families who were divorcing or separating. The following are some of the ones I personally knew:

Couple no. 1 – Togetherness

They sat together in comfortable unison in a darkened venue, watching the stage filled with whirling and leaping figures. She was blonde, healthy looking and very pretty. He was tall, dark and handsome and together they unintentionally achieved a celebrity-like presence. Why did they ever split up? This couple lived together in a Georgian house in Highgate Road, NW5, and round the corner from the next couple who lived in Croftdown Road, NW5.

Couple no. 2 – Humour

He made her laugh from morning till night and they shared so many common interests like looking at life with their 'non-politically correct views' on all kinds of people and events.

In those days this type of humour was not stigmatised.

After he ran off with his secretary (stereotypically,) his wife's laughter died down and she consequentially went to see many comedy shows for some necessary healing.

Couple No. 3 – A Bright Start

This couple were stunning and stylishly turned out. In contrast to how attentive they were to their appearance I do remember their house always looking scruffy and unkempt. Their personalities definitely lit up any party or gathering and their children were complete mirror images of themselves. This couple lived in a large roomy house off Essex Road in Islington, N1.

He however, was not so stereotypical and ran off with a stripper from Soho.

Couple no. 4 – Loving homes filled with loving children

"He must be mad to leave his family and wonderful home!" said his best mate, who three months later paralleled his best mate by leaving his family and lovely home, to run off and live in Hollywood as well but his choice was with a 'Charlie's Angel.' They lived in Acacia Road in St. John's Wood, NW8 in a grand and immaculate looking house just around the corner from 'Arnold House School' which Josh and this particular couple's son attended.

Couple no. 5 – In the name of spirituality
At the same time, another friend ran off to be an 'Orange Person' which is a 'Rajneesh' follower and he also left his family and home. In the name of spirituality the 'Rajneesh' cult got a hold of this friend and he left his two children and wife to go and live in a spiritually dubious Ashram in 'Upstate' New York.

Couple no. 6 – Exotica
Some other friends of mine had a rich and exotic lifestyle that took them worldwide. All was going well on the surface and then suddenly he disappeared from England and the reason for this has still not yet come to light. They lived in the North London suburbs of Mill Hill in an exceedingly rich setting.

These separations and ugly divorces happened within months of each other to close knit friends who on the outset looked right and happy together and set up for life.

A disconnecting holocaust hit NW London!! Therefore things obviously were not quite as they seemed.

Chapter Three

LONDON IN THE 80's

'adness' were a local band that became very famous in the early
80's. Their music videos, e.g. 'House of Fun' and 'Baggy Trousers'
were filmed around the Kentish Town area and many local boys
took part and appeared in the videos. Many friends and members of
Madness went to schools in the area, for example Haverstock Hill, William
Ellis and Ackland Burghley.

The year was 1984 and just when one wondered what the next fashion
statement or subculture, hopefully involving a new dance, would be, along
came the craze... 'Breakdance!'

Two breakdance films came out on screens all over the country. These
were 'Beat Street' which captured some of the music and overall birth of
the scene with its foundations being rooted on the streets of the South
Bronx in New York City and also the film 'Breakdance' which came from
the West side of America, in Los Angeles and had a different version of
breakdancing. That film also showed a bit more 'popping' and 'locking'
which was the less physical, not on the floor dance but had more of the
'Michael Jackson' feel.

Josh used to go to a club on Oxford Street called 'Spats!' This was the
place where all the best breakdancers of London would go and he would tell
me that the atmosphere was as John Travolta once said 'electrifying!'
(Quoted from the film 'Saturday Night Fever.')

After the club Spats, where 'Breakers' would be non-stop spinning for a solid 3 hours every Saturday, many would leave to see what was 'cooking' or (going on) in Covent Garden. There would be about 200 Breakdancers, plus the crowd with huge strips of lino and ghetto-blasters that were situated in various parts of Covent Garden.

There were also 'Jams' and 'Battles' which were breakdancing competitions between various breaking 'crews' at clubs such as 'limelight' in the West End and the 'Electric Ballroom' in Camden Town.

This phase did not last long and after about a year, in which time almost all schools and cities got excited about this subculture that involved fashion, dancing, old school Hip Hop music and graffiti on the trains and walls, the scene was over.

In New York and London the powers that be made what most people thought was a beautiful expression in Artwork and dance illegal.

I believe this was the last nation sweeping, clearly visible sub-culture that involved every element: fashion, music, dance, and even artwork.

This decade also brought about the birth of the 'Yuppie' (young, up and coming person) during the reign of Margaret Thatcher or as was commonly known, the 'Iron Lady.' This was also the age when mobile phones and fax machines were introduced, which were ideal accessories for any self-professed yuppie.

The Housing Bill Act was brought in by Margaret Thatcher's government, obliging councils to sell their houses and flats to their tenants and it also disallowed the scheme of parents handing down their council property to their children, thus eliminating the indigenous communities all over London. Her fame also increased for her restraint of trade union power and her ridding London of the Greater London Council.

She also fenced off Stonehenge and one now needs permission to enter. I personally remember the total freedom of that place and the many days out there enjoying picnics with family and friends. However the 'Druids' still attend their annual Summer Solstice, despite their initial confrontations with the police when they felt their freedom and respect for the stones was being attacked by the restricting fences. My son Josh and millions of other children wondered where their milk had gone, that used to be served to them at school daily, before she decided to take that away as well.

Margaret Thatcher acted quickly and took on the battle to reclaim the

Falkland Islands after they were invaded by Argentinean Major-General Menendez. Troops and battle ships were sent and once again the Islands were reclaimed and became part of Great Britain. After the war, Margaret Thatcher was greeted by cheering crowds at the entrance to Downing Street and they sang 'For She's a Jolly Good Fellow' 'Rule Britannia' and the 'National Anthem.' Her reply was that 'Great Britain is great again!' On the other hand Ken Livingstone (the leader of the Greater London Council) Arthur Scargill (the leader of the miner's strike) and millions of people and their children would have disagreed with the abolishment of certain housing rights, the ruination of local mining towns in Northern England, the dissolution of the GLC the ban of free milk cartons for children at schools and so much more besides.

The law rejected a ban on giving the pill to those under 16. This was because of a campaign by Miss Victoria Gillick.

The Metropolitan Police announced that some Special Branch Officers would be allowed to carry automatic weapons.

More than 15,000 people protested against plans to build a high-speed rail link for the Channel Tunnel.

The 'Guardian Angels' (a group of New York subway vigilantes) had arrived in London. Much was written and featured about the 'Guardian Angels' in the States. Their group was founded in 1979 by Curtis Siliwa and their object was to patrol crime ridden areas and to offer a feeling of safety. Their first patrols were on subways and streets and I remember when they visited London to instil the same feeling of confidence when commuters travel on the underground. They travelled on certain tube routes and acted as a 'safety' presence for passengers worried about robberies and attacks, hence the 'vigilantes' label. They were distinctive and noticeable looking with their red berets and bomber jackets. For some reason this idea did not last long but for a short time it was a comfort to feel a protective presence whilst travelling under the streets of London.

North West Londoners

Edwina Currie 'Junior Health Minister' at that time resigned in the wake of angry protests from farmers over her claim that most British eggs were infected with Salmonella. She was famous for her offensive statements such as "Northerners die of ignorance and crisps!" "Cervical cancer is the result of being far too sexually active!" and "Good Christian people will not catch AIDS!" Edwina, from Golders Green, North London, said "I have no regrets!"

London Bobbies put charity before formality by wearing red noses which was the symbol of 'Comic Relief.'

A cataclysmic disaster happened when a fire started on a wooden escalator in the underground station at King's Cross. It was presumed the worst fire ever to hit London's underground and arose from a lit cigarette bringing about the death of thirty people. As a result of this disaster, a no-smoking ban was placed on London's underground for all time.

The pleasure boat 'Marchioness' was hit by the dredger 'Bowbell' on the Thames River. Sixty people died on what should have been a night of joy.

Three terrorists seized twenty hostages at the Iranian Embassy, demanding freedom for ninety-one Arabs held in Iran. The 'SAS' stormed the Embassy and managed to free all the hostages.

Unemployment reached 2.5 million; the highest since World war Two.

'Michael Foot,' who lived in Pilgrim's Lane, Hampstead, became the Labour Party's leader and was seen by us and many others frequenting the heath. In fact many famous people live and have lived in the Hampstead area and you might see 'Michael Palin,' famous for 'Monty Python's flying circus' running over the heath or 'Bill Oddie,' from the 'Goodie Show' doing some bird watching or the odd pop star here and there going for a stroll.

'John Hurt' the famous actor who lived in Flask Walk, Hampstead, starred in the film 'The Elephant man.' The public house in Camden Town, on the corner of Camden High Street and Hawley Crescent, where John Merrick (who was the original Elephant Man) used to drink is still there today and is aptly named 'The Elephant's Head.' The sign outside the pub showing the head of an Elephant originated from the Coat of Arms of Marquis Camden, later used on the Borough of Camden's own shield.

'Sir Oswald Mosley,' the Fascist leader in the 1930's and friend of Hitler and Mussolini died.

Hundreds of West Indian youths battled the police during the 'Brixton riots;' black leaders claiming that the riots were the result of years of heavy-handed policing in Brixton.

'John McEnroe' won Wimbledon after beating Bjorn Borg, the tension was nerve-wracking for them and also the millions of fixated viewers.

McEnroe's abusive behaviour on court lost him a third of his £27,000 winnings in court but probably brought him more fame and financial success in the long run. It certainly provided more focus and entertainment than any other undoubtedly less animated tennis match.

'Salman Rushdie' wrote his 'Satanic Verses,' which was considered to be very blasphemous amongst some Muslims. Due to his comments, a 'Fatwa' (a death sentence from the Iranians) was placed upon him and he was forced to hide under Police guard in London and still remains in hiding to this day.

'700 million viewers around the world watched the most popular wedding of 'Prince Charles' and 'Lady Diana Spencer' at 'St. Paul's Cathedral.' Josh still possesses a commemorative mug as part of the memorabilia. Prince Andrew married Sarah Ferguson in the splendid although slightly less viewed wedding in 'Westminster Abbey.'

Seventeen year old Marcus Sarjeant was jailed for five years for firing blanks at the Queen on Pall Mall. The Queen also woke up one morning to find a dishevelled man sitting on her bed in Buckingham Palace. He only wanted a chat and the Queen unwillingly obliged until she was able to summon help and it was amusing for us but probably not for her.

'Sir Ralph Richardson,' the famous actor, died. He was renowned for being a great English eccentric and shortly before his death was seen riding his motor-bike round the beautiful 'Regent's Park' with his pet parrot sitting stereotypically on his shoulder. He was very critical of his own work and also his face, "I've seen better-looking hot-cross buns!" he once announced.

LONDON IN THE 80's
(A MORE PERSONAL ACCOUNT)

SHE DEVIL

Fay Weldon came for lunch soon after my marriage broke down and I was understandably feeling abandoned and vengeful. At that moment I had a kitchen full of noise, fraught with emotion and schools to attend to, with no help, plus the knowledge and thoughts of my ex husband with his 'new wife to be' living it up in first class hotels. I told Fay that I felt like following in a friend's footsteps; dumping the three kids and cat on my ex's doorstep and going away to India for a very long break but I knew and Fay did too that I would never do such a despicable deed ...."Oh the pain of being too moral!"

Later in the year Fay brought out 'The She Devil,' a really good novel based on the revenge of a wife doing the exact same deed I had talked about. It became a best seller and a great film followed and I had a sense of admiration that I had originated the idea.

GROWING UP

Nights out

Fortunately I'm a very good sleeper as on occasion Sophie and Josh would come home, sometimes in the dead of night, from a party that could be held as far away as South London. The journey could quite well take them over Westminster Bridge, along Whitehall, up through the West End and perhaps up Harley Street which leads into Regent's Park. Across the park, they would continue to walk over Primrose Hill, up Haverstock Hill towards Hampstead village, down Pond Street (which is where the Royal Free Hospital is) and onto Hampstead Heath, via the little choo choo train track bridge and across the starlit peaceful night of the green countrified heath. After their serene night-time walk over Hampstead Heath they would finally end their journey home.

Style

At fifteen years old Sophie went off regularly to the 'Camden Palace' with her friend Lucy. They dressed up, wore make-up, high heels and tight skirts and would come home in the early hours after a night's hard dancing.

At sixteen years, there was a re-markably quick change to 'Bovver Boots,' shaven heads and no make-up. This style matched the political views of those times.

Desperate

It was once listed to me all the parks and open spaces where young people squatted down to do the 'No. 1s' and amazingly even the 'No. 2s' whilst returning from the late night venues: Waterlow Park, Highgate Woods, all sides of the heath, the heath extension, Primrose Hill, Parliament Hill, Regent's Park, to name but a few, where these faecal events took place.

Anxiety

I was not so relaxed with my youngest child Charlotte because the climate of safety had been changing over the years due to a troubling escalation of crime and violence.

She once told me of seeing the purple moon behind St. Anne' church at 3am, as she walked down Highgate West Hill and how romantic and mysterious it looked. However, my changed response was "Please! In future get a cab, even if it means missing these poetic sights!"

Run For It

Charlotte attended Paragon Hill School in Hampstead when she was eleven years old and at lunchtimes they were taken to the East side of Hampstead Heath, to let off steam.

Once while straying into the woods, they disturbed somebody's peace. He was stood on a fallen tree trunk with only trainers on, playing with himself and when he saw them he aggressively gave chase and they consequentially ran away. The police were called but by the time they arrived, the disturbed man had disappeared.

Charlotte was vivid in her descriptions of how his 'in between the legs tackle' bounced about and she thankfully laughed all afternoon at the thought of it.

Annoyance

On the way to one of their East Heath outings, the kids would ring 'Boy George's' bell to try and get him to come to the door. They were all big fans. Boy George once told Charlotte's teacher that 'he thought they all attended a mad school and why weren't the children's behaviour kept under better control.'

'From one who is whiter than snow!' I thought.

Tenants

'(*I know Mum doesn't like it when the tenants smuggle someone in for the night but I'm sure I heard voices*') Sophie thought to herself. Then she heard the tenant's door open slowly and Heather's voice whispering to her new boyfriend that the way was not clear because Sophie was sitting on the stairs reading a book.

"You can't leave, not yet!" was whispered at the door as it kept on closing and opening. 'Not yet!' mused Soph.

She then teasingly pondered; 'this is a good book and I might well stay here for another hour at least!'

Idiosyncratic

Heather was our nocturnal tenant and only appeared after around 10pm at night and would then either wander the streets or study motor manuals till dawn.

Unusually whilst out one afternoon, she was taking photos in Hampstead High Street and found herself answering questions from a swarthy young man from Iran. Heather now had a boyfriend. He would appear standing on the wall at the back of the house, looking confused as to why, on a bright sunny day, Heather's curtains were drawn. His dark looks and trespassing caused consternation with the neighbours and specifically scared one who happened to suffer from a nervous disposition and thought she was about to be 'burgled or worse!'

"What do you want?" the neighbour shrieked.

"The beautiful blonde behind the velvet curtains!" he answered.

"Well, there is no-one there by that description (I was obviously no contender) so please go before I call the police!"

Nothing woke Heather and after about three years, no-one had ever known that she lived in my house.

Put down

Being a landlady was one of my sideline occupations and I remember one time, a tenant of mine asked if she could watch TV with the family. My youngest, Charlotte, said "Mummy says you talk too much!" which I thought was a good example of the subtle discretion one sometimes gets from youngsters.

Embarrassing Situation

I often saw a familiar face on the heath and always said "hello," although I could not remember his name. Where did I know him from I asked myself? Was it from yoga or my clubbing days? "How is Sophie?" "How is Josh?" "How is Charlotte?" "How do you know us all so well?" I replied. "I lived in your house as one of your tenants for two years!" he answered.

Alternative guests

One summer, I made some extra money providing 'B & B' for overseas visitors. A professor of Anthropology came from Japan to stay for a few weeks whilst working for the London University. One Saturday afternoon, over tea, Sophie and her friends were talking round the kitchen table and the Professor was accidentally squashed into the corner. Everyone had gathered to discuss their various trips to India and the conversation seemed to centre round dysentery and diarrhoea. The subject matter went into intricate detail and involved its consistencies and hues, also where and when, for how long, recommended recovery remedies, which ones worked and which ones did not.

I left the room and three hours later when I returned, they had not changed their seating positions and neither had the topic of conversation. Another thing that had not changed was the position of the Professor; this involved the entirety of his whole physical demeanour which included the utterance of any vocal sounds emanating from his mouth. I was told later that he had in fact not said a single solitary word.

Ominous

One afternoon, I was being treated to a Chinese lunch in an empty restaurant by a friend and his associate, who was the owner of this successful and unusual Chinese, European mixed establishment.

Sampling various dishes and basking in the over-confident atmosphere of these two men, I to my dismay heard the mention of Arms dealing to an African State. This was big sordid business which left me feeling cold, shocked and sad and with somewhat haste, I was relieved to emerge back into the everyday busy streets of London Town.

Rats

'Scurry! Scurry! Back and forth.'

Sleeping at the top of the house I could hear the rat in the loft overhead and my rest was constantly disturbed. One night I was sitting on the settee around midnight when I heard a noise coming from the chimney and then suddenly out popped a huge rat onto the hearth before it hastily scuttled into the corner of the room. Needless to say I ran out and frantically closed the door tight behind me. The following morning, a female rat catcher arrived from Camden Council, dressed in green overalls and holding a rat catching net. "Stay right behind me!" she declared. (I thought she was more scared than I was.) Then she casually said "If the rat jumps for your neck, don't worry, it's really jumping for the light behind!" "Charming!" I thought. The rat by this time had gone back up the chimney and so we looked for droppings in case of Weil's disease. The next time I phoned the council for a rat catcher, a tall and thin man came round instead. *'He doesn't look much like a rat.'* I thought. This way of thinking occurred because of my ongoing presumption that people take on the looks of their vocation. He looked to me more like a squirrel. "You know what's more of a problem than rats?" he said, "SQUIRRELS!" and then I reluctantly heard long, enthusiastic stories of how damaging squirrels are to greenery and foliage. He continued to say "We are never more than 12ft from a rat in London" and then began to tell me many rat stories. Being so tall he could not get into the loft easily to drop poison and consequently stepped on a pipe leading to my water tank. It frustratingly and annoyingly broke and water cascaded throughout the entire house. Camden Council did have to pay but predictably fell short of £100.00 .....'Typical!'

Of course, I still had my rats and many rat catchers proceeded to come in different shapes and sizes, as did the rats. Finally, in desperation, I smuggled a cat in from the street, which although enjoying snuggling down in my warm loft, was unfortunately ineffective in getting the rats.

After much inspection of the drains, no traces of rats were to be found and a young man, new to the job as rat catcher had the bright idea that it might be a problem coming from further up the street, where the rat might be entering via a manhole and being that my house was the end house, the rat made its arrival because it could go no further. His presumption made sense.

A manhole cover was replaced up the street and the rat problem became finally and thankfully over.

Chapter Four

LONDON IN THE 1990's

C ocaine was becoming increasingly popular amongst the music and fashion world and even in the finance district of the City of London. Ecstasy and dope were also becoming ever more popular, especially amongst teenagers and the youth.

Image and beauty was playing a more essential part of the music industry than sheer natural talent and there was a bigger leaning towards American culture such as hip hop which started influencing even language and accents primarily amongst the youth. The 90's also brought in a more novel version of Brit Pop and this was represented by bands like Oasis, Blur, Pulp and solo artist Robbie Williams. The 'Spice Girls' all female pop group went to No. 1 with their debut single 'Wannabe' and beat the other major competitors Oasis and Blur.

The Scottish film 'Trainspotting' starring Ewen Macgregor, represented a seedy and destructive side of the heroin culture and it also put Ewen Macgregor on the fame map.

Politically, John Major won the battle to become Britain's new Prime Minister in 1990. At 47 he was the youngest Prime Minister this century has had and his first task was to unite the Tories after the purple-clad Margaret Thatcher tearfully left 10 Downing Street and a disenfranchised conservative party.

Fine powdery snow was blamed for the failure of British Rail's new trains not running on time.

Lord Nolen presented his report on the 'standards of public life' aimed at cleaning up 'sleaze' in the Westminster corridors of power. Did it work?

The Government banned the sale of meat from the section of flesh along backbones of cattle in order to reduce the risk of exposing humans to 'mad cow disease.'

Princess Diana gave her famous candid interview to BBC One's 'Panorama' and was very frank about her private life. In particular, she mentioned James Hewitt with whom she had an extramarital affair and said "Yes I adored him; yes, I was in love with him." Her comments on the constitution and the Prince of Wales caused upset amongst the Royal relations but Diana said she believed that though she would never be "Queen of Britain!" she hoped to be the "Queen of people's hearts." She felt a lack of sympathy for her eating disorder and also remarked on there being "three people in her marriage!" After the interview, Princess Diana agreed to divorce Prince Charles and at around the same time Prince Andrew and his wife Sarah Ferguson, the Duke and Duchess of York also became divorced.

The United Kingdom and much of the world were in grief at the news that Diana 'Princess of Wales' had died in a car crash in Paris. The funeral took place at Westminster Abbey and about a million turned out to line the streets to pay tribute to her. Countless people were throwing innumerable floral bouquets at the hearse as it travelled through London.

Princess Diana's Funeral
Walking through the empty streets of Hampstead, down Arkwright Road to Finchley Road and joining the large crowds to see the hearse carrying Diana's coffin, on her journey northwards to 'Althorpe' (her former family home.) Many locals turned out, as they do on these special occasions and many a 'left wing' and 'anti royal' eye was moistened with emotion.

Gay Times
This was a time when the gay scene made their presence felt and five homosexual couples were married in Trafalgar Square at a Gay Rights Demonstration.

Freddie Mercury, the lead singer of the famous rock group 'Queen' died from Aids. Benny Hill, the comic genius was loved worldwide and died of a heart attack in his London home. The British artist Francis Bacon also died and was a renowned face around the restaurants and bars of Soho (which also has a gay area on Old Compton Street.)

For the very first time shops were opened legally on Sundays and thousands responded enthusiastically (as they predictably always do!)

Oscar Wilde, who died in 1900, was admitted to Poet's corner in Westminster Abbey in the form of a commemoration window.

'New Labour' came to power with Tony Blair as the new Prime Minister and at 43 replaced John Major for the youngest Prime Minister competition.

In 1991, due to public opinion and unrest, the council tax replaced the previous poll tax. Poll Tax is a 'per person' head tax and became very unpopular after it was levied by Margaret Thatcher. The system seemed to shift the tax burden from rich to poor as each person per household was taxed. The protest riot in Trafalgar Square kicked off in 1990 and this unrest was instrumental in toppling Margaret Thatcher and her successor, John Major, into replacing the poll tax with the Council Tax system.

Environmentalists also attacked the government for proposing to spend £13.4 billion pounds on new motorways thus erasing more of what was once the beautiful English countryside.

Customs officials seized an unbelievable big haul of 116lbs of heroin which was to date the biggest ever haul in Britain.

IRA bombs damaged the 'Carlton Club,' a haunt for Tory MP's, London Stock Exchange brokers and the like.

'Institutional racism' was founded because of the situation when the black teenager Stephen Laurence was murdered in Elton S.E. London. Large complaints were inevitably made at how the police handled this matter.

LONDON IN THE 90's
(A MORE PERSONAL ACCOUNT)

WOMEN OF NORTH WEST LONDON

Plenty to say

The Women: Writers, teachers, an actress, social workers, an Alexander teacher, an exotic hat maker, a well known portrait painter, a café owner, a B & B proprietor, a removal business owner, a lawyer and a clothes designer who made various garments for all the women. The women in North West London are a lively bunch. All very confident, verbally energetic and with their fingers on the hub of life, especially when it comes to sorting out all kinds of problems or dealing with unfortunate crises.

They could be seen with their children and dogs going across Parliament Hill Fields on Hampstead Heath. Their children were always involved with local interests and crazes and the children of these women were also expected to achieve well in life. The women hardly paused for breath with their innumerable opinions and it was exhilarating to spend an evening in their company and despite having to find the energy to retain focus, the dialogue never became boring.

Topics that would be discussed: Marriage, lovers, affairs, toy boys, sex, sex problems, conception, contraception, births, miscarriages, abortion, illness, hormones, the menopause, which method of HRT to take, or shall we go it the natural way? Which Doctor is sympathetic? Which book to read and trust? Do you know what they recommend in America? The talk could continue into education, jobs, careers, home-making, children at schools, which schools, teenagers, children leaving home, grandchildren, changing friendships, falling out, making up, travel, moving house, leaving the country and much more. More often than not the never ending problem of how to lose weight was mentioned: Which diet? Which gym/health club? Swimming pool etc.?

A witty response I once heard was "Try the outdoor ladies pond in winter, it burns up calories and it's better than an orgasm!"

These North West London women certainly made a difference to life itself with their enlivened minds and their capacity for sharing, not just socially but more importantly at those times when friends were in need.

Pensions and retirement still yet to come and concluding discussions on old age and death? .... "Never!"

TIME AWAY

A group of my North West London friends decided to get away from the rigmarole and busy polluted streets of inner city life so my friend Zena suggested we join the 'Native American Indians' on a camping trip to the Colorado mountains which seemed to be about as much as an opposite change as we could have imagined.

We then drove across enormous plains which were once inhabited by the 'ponied' Indians and Buffaloes and our Indian guide requested we set up camp by a large river in the

National Park and we also authentically slept in Wigwams. The desert at night became freezing and as I lay in my sleeping bag looking towards the top-most point of the Wigwam, I noticed a hole revealing a crystal pure view of the very clear starlit sky which was an utterly different and profoundly enriching experience compared to the polluted nightly sights back home in the metropolis.

We spent hours building a 'Sweat Lodge' and inside the heat was sauna like and we called up the Spirits in true original Indian style! Hot coals from a fire outside were taken to a hole in the ground inside the sweat lodge and herb-infused water was poured on. After some incantations from 'Dennis' our Indian guide, we would start sweating and only a few people could take more than two rounds of this intensely hot treatment. Afterwards we would clamber out into the cool mountain air and I felt twenty years younger, as well as being 'high as a kite!'

The well used outside wall

The boys sat on the wall outside our front door to talk and smoke, whatever the evening or season.

F##ck, sh##t, c##t and other words were often repeated in their endless, scintillating conversations; I never did catch the bits in between. Behind the very same wall, the postmen hid their large grey bags for them to pick up later and the local window cleaner hid his spare bucket there as well.

An old lady would often sit there to rest whilst on her way to and from the nearby shops.

The cats from the neighbourhood used to go behind the wall to relieve themselves and a dog from next door would also pee profusely until one day I pointed out to the dog's owner that "nobody from my house would urinate on your wall!"

SECOND TIME AROUND

One Night Stand

The bar was dark. Later that night, the young man's room was even darker and I barely noticed his one bed, one suit, one shirt, one spare pair of shoes and no wardrobe. I then remembered my ex-husband's line of expensive suits and 'forty two pairs of shoes!' We proceeded to puff on a joint which was fairly tedious and consequentially spoke little. After what seemed like hours it became time to leave and I gratefully descended the stairs.

Dark once again, down and down I went from way above a grocer's shop without being escorted. Due to no light I found the setting spooky and a little fearful but I eventually found the street door. As I skirted round some boxes to get to my car, I could make out the shapes and hear the mutterings of the early morning delivery men. I did not want to be seen and I came to the conclusion that this way of passing time was not for me!

Looking for a Man

Boldly place an ad or answer an ad. Here's an interesting one I thought; Gabriel, he's Jewish, likes yoga and sounds rather or hopefully attractive. He walked towards me and thus far looked nice and so off we went for dinner at the local curry house. The funny thing (which occurred to me as the evening wore on) was that this particular restaurant had already been frequented before many times by me with some of my male friends. Realising this I felt somewhat embarrassed as I thought the gazing staff might presume that I was 'on the game!' Nevertheless, this particular date decided he wanted to go off to live with his Guru on a hillside in Sri Lanka, commit to a vow of celibacy and finally to reject all notions of a relationship. Somewhat ironic to go to all those lengths just to tell me that!

One year later, he turned up dressed in stereotypically Indian yogi, hippy style gear (long beard, extremely long straggly hair, pink balloon pants, rainbow coloured hat, complete with the inevitable alternative-stating sandals.) Walking beside him, with his dimmed, in disguise looking glasses through Hampstead High Street, I came again to the conclusion that this was not for me!

Chat Up Lines

"What do you think of Tantric sex? Yoga and sex? Isn't yoga meant to increase your libido? It all sounds so interesting; could I have your phone no.?" These are just some enquiries into the 'spiritual' aspects of yoga and that maybe this could be my reason to pursue my profession as a yoga teacher!

I've also met very young men at clubs, who look at me as if to say 'single parent – failed desperado!' Then there are those men who are on the opposite side of the spectrum and want a ready made family and of course to complete it all, there are your trusty cheating married men!

These are all thankfully not for me!

Ageism
The young man was looking interested whilst overhearing a conversation that I had three grown up children and after hearing this piece of information, he started scrutinising my neck to look for evidence of old age.

Reminiscing Mum
Years ago, I tried walking up Hampstead High Street in my 60's thigh-high suede boots to see if they still had the same effect. In my youth, my natural suppleness and unconscious strength stopped me feeling how uncomfortable and physiologically awkward these boots really were. Being misplaced as far as time, era, and age were concerned, these boots have now been relegated to a retrospective shop on Portobello Road, West London.

'These boots were made for walking!'
'Hopefully they will out walk the times I used them in the 60's and, I presume, by someone who is not my present age, else she could be seen as a 'walking embarrassment!'

Missed
Gunnel had moved to London from Sweden in the early 60's and felt liberated. She was well known and popular for her lively sense of humour and her black gloved, gesticulating hands that she waved around, to hopefully draw attention from some of the local men who no doubt were regulars at the Richard Steele's pub on Haverstock Hill, the Robert Peel pub on Queen's Crescent, the Monarch pub and the Marathon bar on Chalk Farm Road. These were some of her passing haunts, usually at some unearthly hour, after an indulgent night out somewhere.

After a long time of this kind of life, she changed course, became a 'Born Again Christian!' went off to Ghana and was never ever seen again in those lively, sometimes crazy, often very musical North-West London old haunts.

Get Fit

Out at an all night rave at Bagley's (a massive warehouse-type venue in King's Cross) to dance non-stop to House, Garage and Trance music. I decided to drink water all night and used that experience as a work-out. During my dancing to the music, a dread-locked figure appeared from the shadows and slowly moved towards me.

"Would you like some speed?"

"No thanks!" I replied and he disappeared back into the shadows. Later he came out again. "Would you like some cocaine?"

"Oh, no thanks!"

Next time he came by, he asked me "would you like some weed?"

"Oh, no thanks!"

Finally he stepped forward. "Are you completely straight?"

The answer was a resounding "Yes!"

Chapter Five

ANIMAL FARM

It's a Dog's life!

It certainly is! There seems to be an ever growing trend to look after, nurture and honour our four legged friend. In the early 60's I never saw any dogs on the Heath or at Kenwood but now almost everyone owns two, three or more. The dog has often been bought to give the owner some exercise (or so I'm told!) but instead you can see them standing watching their dogs leap and bound through the undergrowth and race between people's legs. Observe the face of a dog owner light up when the dog has leapt ahead and then returns and hear them intelligently say "What a clever boy you are!"

Glowing Admiration

The latest I heard is that there is now a 'dog's crèche!' What next? Maybe they should give them an IQ test and send them to prep school, along with a briefcase for all their schoolwork before they return home for an intense game of chess!

Slim and Trim

He bought himself a lovely dog to help him lose weight and keep him company with his incredibly slow walking on Hampstead Heath. At first all went well and he surprisingly avoided the local pub and then I noticed sometime later that the dog was always with somebody else whilst this particular owner sat back on the couch and resumed his much needed munching and daytime television programme viewing!

Extra Cash

How much to walk dogs? What is the going rate? Around £5/6 per hour but is there a limit on how many dogs can be walked at any one time? I'm told it is at least nine or ten which is not a bad wage for defecating over what was once 'God's good clean earth!'

Shaken Up

A black bullet of a dog shot out from the pack and threw me up in the air and I landed heavily. Even though I was bruised and shaken for weeks, the owner had not observed this incident due to being busily occupied and sub-consciously self-important on her mobile phone!

Chapter Six

HAMPSTEAD HEATH

All Weathers

T hink of all those conversations the trees have listened to over the centuries; how many problems that have tried to be rectified, the many love affairs that have started and ended and all the gossip of the many lives that are in London.

Famous People

One of the most incredible and astounding things I've noticed about Hampstead Heath are the footsteps of all the famous writers that have trod its paths, throughout the ages. For example; Keats, Coleridge, Dickens, Blake, Thomas Hardy, Robert Louis Stevenson, D.H. Lawrence, Daphne Du Maurier, Oscar Wilde and probably more that I am not aware of. There are also famous people from all walks of life and Hampstead carries on this reputable nature to this day, housing those such as Michael Foot, Noel Gallagher, Victoria Wood, Michael Palin, Charles Dance, Esther Ranzen, Boy George, George Michael, Jonathan Ross and Bill Oddie to name but a few.

I wonder if Hampstead Heath has founded more inspiration rather than just merely going for a physical enhancing walk!

There are many plaques of famous people who have lived in the Hampstead area like 'Keats, D.H. Lawrence' and many more besides.

A Well Recommended Walk

I realise some of my readers will know Hampstead Heath very well and will know that from Highgate Road it is most pleasing to walk up to the top of 'Parliament Hill' and see the best view of London, preferably on a clear day. From there, you walk down the opposite side and continue to where you will find tree-filled paths. A path that goes northwards will lead you to a Victorian Viaduct Bridge which crosses between two picturesque Lilly Ponds; an ideal scene for many a painter. Carry on upwards to Jack Straw's pub and take in the unusual meeting point of various air currents that come from different directions, resulting in a more revitalising and purified air. One of England's most famous painters 'John Constable' painted a scene of this area with the view of Harrow in the background; this incidentally hangs on a wall at Kenwood House which is situated in the Kenwood area of Hampstead Heath. Walk downwards from Jack Straw's Castle along North End Road, past the car park and turn onto a narrow earthy track. Follow this track and you will notice an iron gate 30yards down on the right. This opens into the ornate ivy-cluttered, Victorian looking Pergola. At the other

end of the Pergola you can walk down into Golders Hill Park. Near Golders Hill Park is the Old Bull and Bush pub and Hampstead Way which leads to the heath extension where you will see the best post-card like view of St. Jude's church, which is situated in the heart of Hampstead Garden Suburbs. Then turn around, walk upwards and back through Hampstead Heath woods. On the other side of the wood is Hampstead Lane, cross over and you will soon arrive at the Kenwood Estate where you will find Kenwood House; an impressive Georgian stately home that looks onto English aristocratic-like grounds. Kenwood House has an old-fashioned art gallery and next door, a Brew House for a well deserved cup of tea. Leaving from the left hand side of Kenwood you will wind downwards and pass a rather obscure looking, iron intensified, and old water fountain. Moving onwards, you will finally arrive at the various ponds, some are for fishing and others are for swimming.

This is undoubtedly a worthwhile, inspiring, lavishly scenic walk.

Looks are Deceiving

The man approaching me in Highgate Woods was behaving oddly. He was shiftily looking all around, making me feel very suspicious and 'Rapist' alarm bells were sounding off in my head. Nobody else was of course in sight, only the numerous trees and bushes and with much trepidation I began thinking of strategies to get away, as he was getting nearer. What to do? My knees were hurting and I knew I couldn't run for it. After this state of panic I noticed a pair of binoculars hanging round his neck and at the same time I heard, as if for the first time, the whistling melodies from the birds.

Nature

Whilst enjoying one of my breakfast 'get togethers' with friend Yana (who looks after us with her healing acupuncture) I noticed the red robin sitting on the seat next to me on the terrace of Kenwood House café fly off. I put a small piece of toast on the seat and the aware robin descended to pick up his snack and then again flew off. Soon afterwards I heard the most graceful notes coming from a nearby bush and I appreciatively received a sweet, joyous, humming thank you!

Detrimental Enjoyment

One afternoon I was walking by the ponds on the right side of the heath when I saw some boys fighting.

Rolling about, shoes off and thrown afar, jacket pulled off and into the mud and then some serious punching and kicking, as the victim lay on the ground. These were 'William Ellis' boys and I felt sorry for the obvious misfit who was singled out. I watched for long enough however and discovered that this boy was only serving his time and when he was eventually allowed up, it became time for the next boy to be assaulted.

Not much fun, I thought!

Summer Delights

The ladies' pond is a peaceful haven, very enclosed in its setting with prolific verdure. There is much wild life and often a Heron is sitting in this enclosure, so still he could indeed be mistaken for a statue. One time when I was swimming on my back, he flew overhead and covered me like a cloud. Another time I swam amidst a procession of ducks and it seemed they mistook me for one of them.

At times the peace of the ladies' pond is disturbed by the sounds of crunching apples and the chomping of crisps but it is not too much cause for complaint, alas!

One very crowded and yet surprisingly quiet day (no apples or crisps) a young man accidentally jumped over the railings and soon realised his mistake. He could not jump back quickly, due to the slope of the bank but nevertheless tried his best. At that moment one of the female lifeguards began to yell and scream "GET OUT! What do you think you are doing, this is a women's only area!" This made the young man even more flustered and after finally scrambling himself over the railings and arriving safely on the other side, he turned. "Madam!"

"What!" was the shrieked response?

"You are a bitch!" he shouted and off he went towards Kenwood.

Other Centuries

One day, whilst visiting Kenwood House with a friend admiring the extravagant décor and paintings, I happened to say that I would have liked to have lived in the 18th century as I find it induces a feeling of romance.

Back in Time

Nicholas Wood, a local man of many talents, asked me to star in his film 'The Life of Keats' as Fanny Brawne, who was the love of Keats life.

It wasn't until Nick Wood met my then husband Ariel Levy that he became really excited and began to glow with true creative animation. "Keats," he said, "it must be a reincarnation, the likeness is so startling."

We soon learned that Nick, who was to be our future director, was a man of invention who could make anything out of nothing and have it end up looking more original than the original.

We were invited round to dinner later that week to try on the costumes which Nick had cut and sewn together. This was after he had perused books on period dress and visited Camden Town Market, where his sagacious eye had found an old overcoat which had been tossed there by an overheated drunk who decided that what with spring and a belly full of Guinness, he would no longer need it. However, Nick gratefully did. A few snips and tucks here and there, the addition of a few big black buttons and it was complete. A white necktie and high collared shirt completed the look and by candlelight Ariel looked truly poetic and his likeness to Keats was definitely startling.

The biggest and most important day was to be spent in Keats house on Keats Grove, Hampstead, where after weeks of negotiating 'Nicollini' (we had nicknamed Nick) had been granted permission to finally film.

"No giggling, good performances!" he adamantly declared, as this would be his one day's permitted opportunity to get those valuable shots. Nicollini's tenacity was quite daunting and we hoped we could meet his expectations. He never once seemed to doubt our contributory potential although we would have graciously stepped down for others to fill our shoes. He was always patient and encouraging, except when it came to our giggling.

Another fellow actor joined us on that day, Simon Carey; a big hearty looking fellow who had been cast as Coleridge, Keat's closest friend and helpmate. He joined us looking most elegant, adorned in a hired costume consisting of a brightly coloured jacket and embroidered waistcoat.

At £6.00 per day to hire Keats' house, Nicollini told us not to waste a minute.

The first scene was of me mincing in my tight dress down Keats grove towards my beloved in my usual knees together fashion and I wondered why on this occasion Keats looked physically stiff and distinctly tense. However, he was only trying to conceal the plaque of 'Keats House' with his shoulder. I then proceeded to give him a brief kiss on the cheek before venturing through a gate and into the garden which looked beautifully in bloom and gave the scene some authentically historical atmosphere.

Inside the house a disaster happened because after having organised us in a comfortable circle for a 'tête á tête' and tea, Nicollini discovered that the shutter on his camera was only operating at half speed.

"There's no other day available!" said Nicollini through tears of impotent rage. Therefore to compensate for this we had to perform our actions in slow motion. This proved difficult as we unnaturally, slowly raised our teacups, mouthed our words and received Simon's witty conversation about finding wild boars and kittens amongst the primroses. Later I was patting Keat's fevered brow as he lay on a chaise longue in the drawing room but this unfortunately and comically looked on film as though I was beating him in an angered frenzy.

After this unintentional comedy scene we left Ariel reclining while some visitors began arriving to see the house. We wondered what they would think or perhaps say on seeing him laid out in full attire. "Gee look honey, a wax model of Keats." They laughed somewhat nervously when Keats smirked as he steadily began blinking his eyes open.

A figure came round the house towards us. She was Johanna Richardson of Hampstead who had written a biography on Keats and was most interested to see how we were tackling his life on film. "He never sported a moustache, in fact nobody did in those days, and it only became fashionable much later," we were specifically told. Nicollini replied that this was not too serious a film and therefore did not have to be that scrupulously authentic. This helped to assuage my guilty feelings at perhaps not helping Nicollini achieve his objective.

Nick's wife, Sarah, also played her part as a wanton country woman and shared a romantic scene with Keats in the hay.

Now comes the dramatic ending to the whole film when Keats leaves England and Fanny to set sail for Italy to die of consumption. The next day at home found Nicollini gazing into clear blue skies whilst simultaneously praying for rain. For this scene I was to wave from inside the house weeping into my lace hanky and mournfully watch Keats outside bidding his heavy hearted 'adieus' through the pouring rain.

Cursing the beautiful weather which was freezing yet sunny, Nicollini racked his brains until with his talent for improvisation he came up with a solution. "Do you have a hosepipe?"

"Oh no!" groaned poor Ariel realising at once his intended fate. Who should hold the hosepipe? Our daughter Sophie tried but it proved impossible as her brother became indignant and also wanted to help. The solution was for Ariel to hold the hosepipe himself, as far away from him as was possible, so that it was out of shot. Then, by judicious thumb work over the nozzle, to direct a spray of cold water upwards in order to allow it to cascade 'a la rain' over him. Such a spectacle seen from the warmth within the house of cavorting Keats in the garden, with left arm outstretched and right arm waving in valediction, with a strained countenance, resulted in the director and leading lady unable to control their laughter. Drying himself off later Ariel was relieved to learn that his acting days were finally over.

The film was shown at the 1977 Jubilee Festival at the Everyman cinema, situated at the top of Hampstead. The Barrow Poets (who were local poets) read poetry from the stage in front of the screen as an introductory measure before the main viewing. The film had far more atmosphere than I had anticipated and so basically 'hats off' to Nick for what I thought turned out to be excellent film work, even though alas this was to be its only viewing to date.

Ladies Beware

One morning on a lonely path by the Vale of Health, having just passed the pond on the left, a very unsavoury character was masturbating behind a tree. It was nothing short of gross and spoilt the tranquillity and beauty that we had just prior to experienced. Gratefully I was with a male companion and so did not feel threatened but it took a good deal more walking to rid myself of that perverted image.

More of the Same

Another time I was walking with friends Gunnel and Marlene when we saw a young man directly in front of us with his pants down doing the same five knuckle shuffle.

I have trodden the pathways of Hampstead Heath for many years and am pleased to report that gratefully this type of incident has been rare.

On the Wing

There are also many types of birds, such as Kingfishers, roaming the heath as Bill Oddie, with his binoculars would undoubtedly testify.

Chapter Seven

YOGA

On Time

P ushing and rushing in because the front door always closes dead on time for the beginning of the class. Some of the students can be seen running down the street and round the corner and some anxiously phone to say they are on their way.

Reasons for being late or not coming at all are: Road works, flu, children ill, children playing in concerts, aching joints, feeling dizzy and countless more.

Unusual reasons crop up every now and then: someone having a pain in the nose and, what I thought was extremely amusing was one woman being late because she happened to be belting an unsuccessful mugger over the head with a rolled up yoga mat!

Bright Eyes

After two hours of yoga, some of the students hang around to have a cup of 'chai-masala' tea. This is made from 'Tetley's tea bags, cardamom pods, cinnamon sticks, cloves, fresh ginger, whole black peppercorns and rounded off nicely with milk and honey or Demerara sugar.' After sampling this delicious concoction, everyone's eyes shine and they leave my house full of much needed energy and ready to fight another day in our very fast-paced city.

Aristocrat

Lord Phillimore was very tall, thin and eccentric looking in his definitively checked-tweed jacket, striped trousers and an individualistic red bow tie. Sometimes as an alternative he would wear a less revealing cravat of many colours. One time he phoned up and asked "What should I wear for yoga?"

"A pair of shorts" I answered.

"Oh no!" he said, "I could not possibly let you see my legs!" So he went to M & S for a pair of track suit bottoms which went halfway up his calves, restating his completely natural way of looking out of the ordinary. He would arrive for his 'private' yoga class in his oversized Range Rover with only four dogs in the back! His manner was always charming and amicable and I really did enjoy his visits. On one occasion, he asked me where he could exercise his dogs. "Hampstead Heath is just around the corner" I said.

"Oh no!" he said" not anywhere Bourgeois!" He always forgot to pay me and when eventually I did get a cheque from him, it was for quite a large amount. I noticed the cashier suspiciously looking at me when I deposited the cheque into the bank, as I suppose even so much as meeting a Lord is not really a common occurrence.

He called me the "the lady in the cottage," although most people found my house very large. Unfortunately in one of our conversations however, he did not take the subtle hint to accept my group into his stately home for a yoga weekend.

He found the yoga highly unusual and it did help him emotionally and of course made him supple too. I liked him and his eccentric ways but I did not know him for too long because sadly he died. His lifestyle, which he was desperately trying to alter, had sadly taken its toll.

Full House

 The three year old boy, who lived next door, saw many people enter my house for their yoga class. "Everybody lives in your house!" he shouted and another time he curiously said "you get loads of visitors!"

Being Prepared

The two young men walked from Camden Town to Parliament Hill Fields for their first ever yoga lesson. Once in the hallway they were asked to remove their trainers as is customary. Sweaty feet emerged and it was annoying to see marks on the stair carpet, so I told them to take their socks off and the response was "NOT THAT!" Dirt along with sweat and in the end they became so embarrassed they decided to run off to the bathroom to urgently wash their feet.

Not an ideal student

Joe was tall, lanky and stooped and said "yoga for my posture – no way! All that stretching and bending this way and that and all those boring breathing exercises, I think I'd rather just chill out and puff on a spliff!"

Not Needed

David strode across the heath to his job as surgeon at the Royal Free

Hospital on Pond Street, NW3. Upon long legs with long strides, he walked on through the endless stretch of corridors, day after day.

His gluteus muscles and those on his inner thighs were worked on acutely but he felt more comfortable standing up and never felt the need to come to yoga.

Planning Ahead

On the downward escalator at Sainsbury's Camden Town, I was working out in my mind what programme to give my yoga students later on that evening. I pondered on the dynamic 'warrior' poses and my leg began inadvertently stretching out behind me. My foot collided with something and when I turned round, I realised it was a man' crotch.

"Sorry!" I said.

"Don't worry" he replied, "Nothing is broken."

Chapter Eight

HAPPENINGS

Street Wise

John drank heavily and lived on the streets of Kentish Town and Camden Town. He was a lively character who was involved with crime and often visited prison for short and sometimes long spells. After ten years of this repetitive scenario, in one of his clearer and calmer moments, he thought he would visit his old Mum in King's Cross again.

"Hello John!" she said, when he arrived at her door. "I thought you were dead, come in!"

Thirsty Work

On a long walk through Hampstead's back streets, I and my companion finally reached the area of Golders Green. On passing the gates of Golders' Green Crematorium we saw a sign which said 'TEAS' and so we decided to take a break. I opened the door and about ten pale, wan faces were sat at a table, very quiet and dressed all in black. They looked like they were entrants for a Dracula school but we were actually not far off in our conjecture because they happened to be involved in the coffin trade! I remember distinctly how we could both truthfully feel and smell death from the tea itself, so we decided with somewhat urgency to return back to the land of the living and exited fairly quickly toward the High Street which was far less ghoulish.

Unexpected Meetings

Shopping, or just walking in Hampstead High Street, it is possible to brush shoulders with the rich and famous. One morning I arrived at the 'Coffee Cup' with Charlotte. Looking at our usual seats outside, I noticed Helena Bonham Carter and Charlotte's reaction was to almost freeze at the thought of having to sit next to her. Charlotte is a huge fan and I could see her struggling for composure. Helena must have noticed, as she leaned across to clear her bags and put her cigarette out in the ashtray in front of her.

This unusual encounter ended with the exchange of a few pleasant words.

Alternative Lifestyles

In Croftdown Road, NW5, the builders were paving the patio floor and I made them a cup of tea to wash down the currant-filled Eccles cakes. Looking in my cupboard, I only had Lapsang Soochong tea, goats milk and muscovado sugar.

I listened for complaints or confused sentiments but all I heard was silence.

Born to Live

After years of emotional turmoil and never a dull moment, she often wondered why she had such an extraordinarily dramatic life and was told this was due to her sun being in Aquarius, Gemini rising, culminating with a dash of Leo.

Her friend's life was hard working and predictable due to the Sun in his Libra and Cancer rising.

Her epitaph will read "What was all that about?"
His will read "Was that all?"

Friends

John, who is well known as a jazz and classical guitarist is so tall, he sometimes suffers from vertigo! With a shock of woolly curls and a classic novel under his arm, he jovially strolls across the heath and religiously has tomatoes on toast for breakfast at Kenwood every morning. All my girl-friends love him.

Don't Look Back

One time I decided to raise money for Christian Aid. At the first door I went to, a voice said "I'm not here!" Anger and swearing was at the next door.

It made me reminisce about the days when the street was alive with running, happy children but it is sadly now looking depressed, bedraggled, with many bells on each door and no welcome.

Bosoms

One day a friend who lived opposite me in Croftdown Road was leaving her house looking very uncomfortable on her way to visit the hospital and when she arrived for her appointment at the Whittington Hospital in Highgate, the doctors there looked puzzled as to why her nipples were so red and sore. Many eyes stared hard and brains ticked and clanked over trying to diagnose what the problem could be. Thus, she left the hospital clutching some soothing ointment and no answer.

It was only on her long walk home that she remembered when she threw away her bra the week before and had bought herself a robust linen dress.

'Cyprus in York Rise'
(the nickname for the local Greek Supermarket)

At 'George's' I had a row, years ago which was probably due to family stress rather than the fact that they did not give me coupons automatically for my purchases.

"Right, that's it. I'm not coming here again!" Later, much later, it became really inconvenient not to be able to nip down to that well stocked shop.

Then sister Suzy came to visit and we just so happen to look alike. I asked her to go to George's on my behalf and gave her my coat to wear. When Suzy returned she said "they are so friendly in that shop!" After that I knew it was safe for me to go back.

Chapter Nine

EXTRAORDINARY HAPPENINGS

Changing Times

In 1963, opposite my flat in St. John's Wood High Street was the News-agent's shop and very early on Sunday morning the delivery boys would meet to collect their newspapers. Guaranteed to be noisy, with names being called out, laughter, affectionate pushing and shoving and basically general liveliness.

In 2007, just around the corner in York Rise, NW5, near Parliament Hill Fields, the delivery boys sit quietly looking down at the ground and seem disunited, as they silently wait for the shop to open.

What happened!

Driven Mad

On the way to Euston Station, a mini cab driver was looking fed up, whilst complaining vociferously about his job. "Thank God I'm not doing this for much longer!" he said with great emphatic relief. "I start my new job in a week," he then expectantly announced.

"What is that? I enquired.

"I'm going to be a taxi driver!"

Think Before you Speak

Once on the way to Paddington to board a train to Devon, I was chatted up by the mini cab driver and by the time we approached the station he was telling me that he would love a holiday away from London and was there any chance he could join me on my trip. I thanked him for the ride and quickly paid the fare!

Shining Star

Friend Janie who lives literally down the road in Kentish Town, was making her way home down Highgate Road one autumn day, relishing the speed and control that she had mastered over her new blue, electric trice from which she derived her mobility. Suddenly her brain slid into slow motion as she realised she was about to collide with some railings. When Janie came round she was lying on the ground looking up at an official looking man who was asking for her personal details and in no time was joined by his colleagues from the fire station that was across the road. After a visit to the Royal Free Hospital, she began bathing in the attention her black eye caused. Over the ensuing weeks, it turned all shades and colours of the rainbow and one day she was asked if she had regretted the whole incident.

"Not at all!" said Janie, "I've always loved men in uniform!"

Someone is Playing Games

There it is, another Camden Refuse truck (originally known as a dustbin van) turning into the road just in front of me! Unable to overtake and with my windows down, due to the scorching heat of the day, there is the inevitable stench of refuse (otherwise known as rubbish) in the air. It's weird how many times these, what could appear as 'set-ups,' happen in one's lifetime!

Dehydrated

Sitting in 'Café Mozart's' which is a pavement café in Swain's Lane, discussing health issues with friends, one of them remarked that the Doctor said "you should drink 3 litres a day."

"Of what – Wine?"

Paranoia

I saw a man through the glass door and he held a long metal rod, sharp at one end and on the other, a metal ball. Feeling a bit cautious after reading the crime statistics in the 'Ham & High,'(which is abbreviated for Hampstead and Highgate and is the local newspaper) I imagined him hitting me on the head with the metal ball and then following through and stabbing me with the other end. I later refreshingly found out it was a device used for unblocking drains by the Water Board.

History Repeats Itself

"Josh, why do you have to dress like a skinhead and look so aggressive? At least don't wear the boots! Sorry, I can't go up Highgate Road with you, as everyone is looking!"

Walking home I remembered when I was 16 years old my mother saying to me that she also would not walk up the village High Street with me, as everyone would be looking. In those days, my hair was bright blue and I wore huge high heels and a skimpy skirt.

What's wrong with that!

North versus South

"What are you doing here Father, at midday, in my sitting room reading the paper? I've just been shopping but was expecting you tonight at dinner time!"

He responded "I was lucky to be let in by your tenant and this is 'dinner time' where I live oop north!"

Major Situations

Many a time a gold Rolls Royce would be parked outside my house in Twisden Road, NW5. In the car would be very flash 'don't mess with me characters,' accompanied by their 'Popsy' girlfriends, who looked dressed to kill and would arrive sometimes as early as 8am. This motley crew would head for the wine bar, 'Boxers,' on the opposite corner of my street which I had heard was run by East End Gangsters. Once I went in there with my sister Janet for a nosy 'let's see' and indeed did feel that I had to keep my head down, so as not to disturb any of the rough and tough looking men. The local residents eventually got together to oust them.

The police came and evicted them but later on the gangsters had defiantly shot a bullet hole through the Chetwynd Road front window and also left notices that read 'TOPLESS BAR LADIES' and 'GAY WAITERS WANTED!' They at least had a sense of humour and thankfully never came back to seek revenge, which reassured me because I was one of the nearest to the premises. The wine bar is now 'Chameli,' a very tasteful Indian Restaurant.

Two years after their eviction, my son accidentally sat next to the leader of the gang in the Grafton Arms pub, on Prince of Wales Road, NW5, Kentish Town. The man said that he had got sent down for storing illegal firearms in a fridge in the wine bar, where the drinks were supposed to be. He then offered Josh a job moving boxes at certain selected times of the day to various warehouses and Josh thanked him but declined and settled on just having a drink with him instead. Who knows where Josh would be if he had accepted that particular career route.

Suspicion

I wondered at the numbers of men all relaxing on the roof terrace above the aforementioned wine bar. It did not look like a gay scene, so why were there no girlfriends?

One day I was busy sweeping up leaves in my backyard, feeling very calm and serene when I heard a loud voice "Hands up your back!" When I neighbourly opened the back gate, there were loads of armed police swarming around, as the men were all escorted and put into the back of waiting blue vans.

Later, I heard that this scene was all to do with drugs.

Disorganisation

I would often hear shouting from the flat opposite my house in Twisden Road and would see furniture literally flying across the room and sometimes through the windows. Uncannily, it was the flat next door to the one that involved the previously dramatic drug raid. Once, in the middle of the night, I heard shuffling feet outside my bedroom window. 'What now?' I thought, and as I looked down I saw about twelve riot police officers with shields and helmets running towards yet another disturbance.

On the balcony opposite was my neighbour dangling his baby towards the pavement below and threatening to drop her. I prayed 'God, not the baby! Please, not the baby!' The riot police had been called out to over-power the father but they could not get through the archway because their shields were almost comically too big.

Thankfully the father was reasoned with and escorted away, whilst the baby was taken indoors.

The baby, again thankfully, turned out to be a fine and healthy looking girl.

Skip Lightly

I placed an old bed against the wall at the front of my house in Croftdown Road, NW5, and thought in time someone in need might take it. Nothing happened and so I went to get help to throw the bed onto the skip opposite. Guilty feelings started to creep in as I hadn't contributed a penny towards the skip and so I retrieved the bed and placed it back against the wall.

Murphy's (a massive local building firm) lorry pulled up and two of his men came to the door and said they would take the bed to the dump, for a 'tenner!' but I only had £6.00 which they accepted and away went the bed.

I re-entered my house hearing lots of laughter behind me before the lorry shot off up the road. Looking out, lo and behold there was my bed, back on the skip.

Mistaken Identity

"There are some really dodgy looking characters sitting in a car outside, they have the window down and I heard one of them say, "She's in there alone!" This is what my tenant said to me late at night when she fearfully entered the front door of my house. I responded with "Right! I'd better get their registration number and phone the police!" I asked my tenant, "Who could it be? Can you describe them?"

She said, "You don't want to see how shifty they look; I'm terrified!"

After sneaking out and skulking down to get the registration number, I phoned Kentish Town Police. "Do you have a Panda car nearby because there are two very dodgy-looking blokes in a car outside my window; not moving and with the engine running? We are two females here alone and they have been there for ages! The registration no. is ......"

The policeman checked on his computer. "Madame, it's alright!"

I hastily replied "What! Why?"

He said "Let's just say, you've never been safer!"

In The Dead Of Night

THUMP! THUMP! THWACK! THWACK! I could hear outside my house.

On went the light and I pushed the window open and shouted out "if this does not stop, I will call the Police!"

Looking down I saw lots of helmets bobbing up and down. In the meantime other lights went on and the thumping and thwacking consequently stopped. I then realised it was the police that were doing the beating. I heard later that a young man, who had been acting suspiciously and was followed by police, resisted arrest when they found him 'looking over' a motorbike in the darkness of my street.

Fear Not

'Innocent' is his name. He is black and a staunch member of the Kentish Town Pentecostal church.

He told me that black people feel really bad when walking down the street because sometimes they are looked at with fear, mistrust and suspicion by white people!

In recent years this must have changed with our multiracial and multicultural society in London. There are so many people nowadays that people don't notice each other in our highly dense population that makes the individual person look inconspicuous.

Bottoms Up

I discovered Sophie's friend, Sylvia, was racy in her descriptions of her reunion with her boyfriend who was fresh out of jail, while overhearing some of their conversation at Charlotte's 8th birthday party.

After Charlotte's birthday I picked up my roll of film that was on the table and took it to be developed at the local Photographer's shop. Collecting them later I wondered whose bottom I was looking at, as well as other compromising positions of a lewd nature. 'Sylvia!' I intuitively thought and later on found it to be confirmed as I had unwittingly picked up her roll of film.

Even though I had used this particular photo shop, which was opposite

Parliament Hill School for Girls for many years, this incident made me feel too embarrassed to use it again.

Opportunism

Back from a stint in Prison, local woman C.......saw armed robbers enter the Chetwynd Road Post Office, round the corner. Quickly following them in, she watched them rob the desk at one side of the shelves and took the advantageous opportunity of filling her bag and coat with goodies from the opposite side. She made sure that she was out of the door before the police had time to arrive and was grateful for other people's dishonesty. She was also very grateful for hundreds of pounds worth of dole cheques, patiently waiting for her on her hallway floor after one of her visits to prison, which she also remarked on as being a "relaxing, holiday camp!"

Appearances Can Be Deceptive

"TED!" said Albert "Don't go out looking like a tramp!"

"I'm only going for a pint of milk and a newspaper – won't be long!"

Down Parkway and in and out of the crowds near Camden Road, Ted saw someone coming towards him who looked at him sternly. 'An old friend?' pondered Ted, although he could not quite recognise him. Getting closer, the man outstretched his arm, which Ted responded to in the same manner and they exchanged a warm handshake.

Something was pressed into his hand and when Ted looked down, there was 50p.

Evil Moments

Sitting on a wall in Tufnell Park, near to the tube station, three teenagers noticed that a door opposite was open and they consequently became curious. They walked over and gingerly pushed the door and, hearing no-one, they ventured in. Upstairs on a bed in a filthy room they saw bits of skin and blood and hair. Feeling completely alarmed and wanting to leave, one of the youngsters noticed a tall cupboard against the wall and opened it; knives fell out, covered in blood and from this sight, they ran outside and leaned across the wall on the other side of the road to get over their sickness. A few minutes passed and then they saw a car pull up and some large aggressive looking blokes got out and entered the same building. Then the teenagers hastily fled. Parents of the teenagers reported this incident to the police but no results or reports ever came back.

Unexpected Love

A truly exceptional occurrence happened when transcendental, hippy looking and laid back Eugene Collier, from Chalk Farm, met with the inspired, classy and wonderfully graceful Tamara Becton from Gospel Oak. It was as though divine intervention had played its part, at an evening class in Primrose Hill, where they both went to learn photography. It was a coming together, souls meeting and uniting, a chemistry that was perfectly unifying and not to be denied. It shook them both up for quite a while but had to be left there due to circumstances, fear, age differences and incompatible lifestyles.

So be it for this lifetime!

Tit for Tat

Caroline's boyfriend Tat died from a drug overdose. His funeral was held at Golders Green Crematorium.

My son, his best mate and his best mate's girlfriend were standing outside waiting for the hearse to arrive. The long black car came by with Caroline, looking very upset and hanging onto her friends who were travelling with her, plus the wreath that was in the form of 'TAT.' Then around thirty or more real life punks turned up to give him a good send off.

As they all moved to the hall where the ceremony was taking place, they noticed an orthodox Jewish party which were saying goodbye to their beloved one in the hall next door. Some of the Rabbis had mouths open wide at the sight of the numerous punks that were there with their mangy dogs and bottles of extremely high strength booze.

Once inside, the Vicar stuttered through his regular sermon; he was surprised at the novel experience of seeing the hall filled with anarchic looking punks. It was a good thing that Tat's musical request in the event of death was not played, as this request was the song 'My Way' but it was not Frank Sinatra's version, it was the slightly less known 'Sex Pistols' version. The Vicar, who was unknowingly let off another novel punk experience, concluded his sermon by announcing "If anyone would like to come to the front, to pay their respects, now is the time!" Suddenly, hysterical weeping and wailing could be heard coming from the back of the hall and a drunken man galvanised himself to the front, to offer his condolences.

"It's terrible what's happened, I just can't believe it, poor old Tat!" the man shrieked.

The other mourners did their best to control their laughter because they knew this drunken man did not in fact know the deceased.

After the ceremony they all went outside to the rear of the crematorium, where the wreath was laid to the ground. Instead of the usual flowers, half-full bottles of high strength cider and cans of Tennant's super were placed beside the wreath, in remembrance of Tat. At pretty much the same time, the Orthodox Jewish party finished their service and were assembled next to our group again. Josh noticed their mouths open like before but this time they were even wider. Hurriedly, the Jewish group got themselves together and hastily left Golders Green Crematorium and maybe their upset tears were not just about the mourning of their friend but of what they saw taking place with the punk service.

The Punks and everybody could not wait to get back to the sending off party that was held at a large squatted church that was next door to Kentish Town's biggest music venue 'the Forum' and away from the formal surrounding of Golders Green Crematorium.

IRRATIONAL FEAR

Creepy

As long as I can remember I have suffered from 'Arachnophobia' and it has stopped me from travelling to locations in the world such as Africa, or living in deep country. This type of phobia is passed on in families and usually via the mother. I even asked my tenants if they were able to dispose of spiders before they moved in and neighbours and workmen were often brought in off the street, if I happened to spot an eight legged friend. Sometimes I would vacuum them up, if they were not too big, but this murderous act made me feel guilty.

Once I asked Danny who is a neighbour in Twisden Road to come in when I thought I saw a huge one run under my sitting room rug. I was totally embarrassed when it turned out to be the fringe around the edge of the rug.

At London Zoo (for any of you fellow 'phobics') there is a friendly spider programme which puts us through a process of cognitive therapy and hypnotherapy to cure our affliction. It has an 80% success rate and at the end of the three hour course, a room full of thirty 'phobics' had their photographs taken of them proudly holding 'Frieda,' the bird eating tarantula from South America.

Keeping Fit

Living near Hampstead Heath and Parliament Hill Fields, we residents are told how lucky we are to have such a large open space on which to keep fit. This includes huge areas for walking, plus the running track and the outdoor swimming pool and ponds.

Metti, who is my present lodger enthusiastically rushed off to make use of the Lido on Parliament Hill Fields and after five Olympic size lengths, she returned with a sense of pride and a somewhat celebratory feeling of nobility.

Chapter Ten

2000 TO PRESENT DAY

In the aftermath of the boy band 'Take That' and the first of the all girl bands the 'Spice Girls,' came evermore groups of a similar theme. Some would come up with an original number of 'three' persons in the group, as opposed to the standardised 'five' persons in one group.

There is the black influenced side of music, the Hip Hop scene and the latest commercial style known as 'R n B!' I would be surprised if it is like the original 'R n B,' as the original many decades ago was a completely different sounding 'music' known as 'rhythm and blues' which involved real instruments. There is also garage and I do not know what that style entails but I cannot wait until the next form comes out, which might be known as 'Garden Shed!'

All these latest styles usually involve synthetic instrumentation and lyrically nothing of any value to the mind and soul of the listener. The lyrics are usually about the same sentimental, drip version of love or a promotion of how hard or promiscuous the performer is or harping on about vanity and materialism.

All profound messages, to beneficially influence the listener, I think you will agree!

There are a few fly by night 'Indie' bands but personally speaking, I am not a blatant enthusiast of the present music and fashion scene because I do not see anything real or meaningful about it. Unlike before, where the scene was dictated by the people and gravitated upwards to the commercial businessmen, nowadays it is the opposite way round and unfortunately I only rarely see the originality, soulful electricity and musicianship, often with meaningful lyrical content, that I used to see.

Trafalgar Square has been pedestrianised and is now a wonderful place for people to sit, in front of one of London's great landmarks, the 'National Gallery.' You can admire one of London's greatest views, featuring other great landmarks such as 'Nelson's Column' and 'Big Ben,' which appears at the other end of Whitehall. 'The London Eye' (the world's largest observation wheel) is now to be found on the South Bank of the river Thames, almost directly facing the 'Houses of Parliament.'

The elegant, plain grey, metallic, without any ornamentation Millennium Bridge can be found opposite St. Paul's Cathedral,' situated in the heart of London and demonstrates the difference between post-millennium architecture and the much more detailed and decorative design of the Victorian bridges and even older periodic bridges and buildings surrounding it.

Tessa Jowell, the Sports Minister, believes that holding the next Olympic Games on London's Docklands would bring London onto the world's stage! I thought that the world famous landmarks and architecture of one or more centuries ago, like Buckingham Palace, Big Ben etc, that attract millions of tourists, had already done that!

Buckingham Palace blushed when a young man stripped off at a royal garden party, hosted by the Queen.

The war on Iraq brought about controversy and was highlighted by a protest march in London in which around one million people turned out. Despite this clear opposition, the Government decided to ignore public opinion and hastened the British troops to join the US army in the invasion of Iraq.

Since then we had the Hutton enquiry into Dr. Kelly's suicide. He was an expert on Weapons of Mass Destruction (WMD) and was thrust into the media spotlight after being identified as the man the government believed was the source for a BBC report on Iraq. He became a key figure in the row between the government and the BBC over claims that Downing Street "sexed up" a dossier on Iraq's weapon capability. Two days after facing MPs he was found dead in a field near his country home.

Thousands of country people also turned out on the streets of Westminster to protest against the ban on Fox Hunting, which they said would change the English country way of life and cause a large amount of people to be out of work. Labour had promised this ban before they came to power and most urban people agreed.

On the South Bank near Tower Bridge, a New Yorker called 'David Blaine' began a self-imposed 44 day fast, while suspended 30ft above the ground in a glass box. Living on only water, this 30yr old magician became a huge attraction and magnetised thousands of onlookers to the South Bank. Most people thought that this stunt was amazing but you always have a few antagonists who eagerly attacked him in the box with golf balls, paint and rotten eggs. As a result, he needed security and police protection and managed to succeed fasting for the entire 44 days.

In 2005 we had the terrorist attacks on our underground and buses. It took a while to feel safe travelling through London and I once saw a woman on the Northern Line using her rosary beads rather frantically.

Most old style traditional pubs have been converted into modern swanky 'gastro wine-bars!' When you enter a pub nowadays you will not find the nicotine ash-tray smelling atmosphere, due to the government passing the no-smoking law, in July 2007.

With the young generation growing up nowadays the London cockney accent has mostly been replaced with an American hip-hop style accent mixed with African and possibly a subtle trace of cockney, left over from the old days.

Regents Park holds the most imposing mosque so far in England. Some Christian churches have been converted into modern apartments for your higher earners, such as the church on the corner of Highgate Road and Chetwynd Road in NW5, currently being renovated and turned into flats. A few other churches have been turned into nightclubs like the large church on Muswell Hill Broadway in North London.

Conclusion

Over these decades, London has changed beyond recognition; going from darkened bridges over the Thames, sometimes lit up by the old 'route-master' double Decker buses and a real 'Dickensian' feel, to a more lit-up environment, as far as modern neon-lighted buildings are concerned and which also contributes to a greater number of shiny reflections on London's Thames river.

I remember rundown houses dilapidated and crumbling, with 'squatters' taking over any empty building. Many householders felt that squatters, by and large, like Gypsies, were not to be trusted and were slovenly in their way of life. I also remember seeing the Police fling filthy mattresses and bags of belongings onto the street in Highgate Road, as a bunch of bedraggled, faded and jaded 'hippies' were ejected out of a house that they had been squatting in.

This supposed social problem was for some young people a need to have their sense of 'freedom' and not be bogged down to the confines of earning a living, which often meant for them a mundane and boring job. Many, also, were known as 'Travellers' and they moved up and down the country in their brightly painted vans, often on their way to various festivals. Later on, this way of life was slowly stamped out beneath the feet of covetous landowners, who disallowed camping on their fields and many people were complaining about the chaos which surrounded these alternative lifestyles. Scenarios increasingly occurred, where headlines would read 'Squatters beneath the feet of developers!' This influenced many newspaper buyers into thinking that whatever decisions the government took would undoubtedly be right!

A wave of popular 'house-buying' crept in, which proved problematic for those in dire circumstances and we now have the 'homeless' sleeping in shop doorways, under bridges and basically on the streets of London.

Twisden Road was shabby and run-down with its indigenous working-class residents unable to afford to 'do-up' their rented homes. As they either died or moved on, the atmosphere changed to one of 'affluence,' as the 'well-heeled,' often young couples moved in and then refurbished and re-designed the interiors of these Victorian cottages.

From the days of the untold bands that played the local pubs and clubs to the internationally renowned arenas and stadiums, there is another new replacement which likewise has caught the attention of millions, be they predominantly pre-pubescent.

What once was music that was played and written by musicians who simultaneously were the performers, to pre-recorded music, through computer and synthesised format, being sung but not being played by a handful or less of handpicked young people by organised businessmen, who incidentally run the 'music industry!'

The arrangement that clearly exists encompasses boy and girl 'bands' who through their looks and 18-25 age bracket, go through choreographed dance routines as they mime the pre-recorded synthesised music. Their careers last shorter and shorter as, like any commercial purchase, it is obviously in the interest of the designer to replace products as frequently as possible for those big as you like profits!

Understandably the main consumers of the 'music today' are aimed at and bought by children up to 16 years of age.

As far as fashion and subculture are concerned, there have been some changes. From the Teddy boys (Teds) in the 50's, to the hippies, mods and 1969 skinheads in the 60's, to the rockers, funksters, punks, 2 Tone skins in the 70's, to the heavy metallists, new romantics and breakdancers in the 80's to the Britpop and maybe a bit of American grunge in the 90's, to what we have today.

Thus, what we have today is a handful of skinheads and mods that can be rarely seen at a ska night somewhere, to the odd glimpse of a rocker, to the youth of today that follow 'what!' Well, more than a few get their hands into some underground scene. You have a few youthful looking punks walking round Camden Town, a few American influenced skateboard-style enthusiasts, to the promotion of the pop industry with its extremely American influence. This trans-Atlantic influence that is highly commercial is not solely for the voices that sing the pop music but is also affecting the clothes that come from manufactured high street designers.

Unlike in previous decades, when the fashion was inspired by subcultures, whose roots are from the streets of major cities, the clothes of today are purchased from high street shops that supply a very non-descript, catalogue style, with a dash of raunchy naughtiness about them!

On a personal note, my children have their own interpretation of life on this planet and with their curious and imaginative minds, they are following a 'trend' to live away from their 'home-town' and are looking to the USA to build their futures, with Sophie already leading the way. She lives in the Venice Beach area of Los Angeles with Ivan from Belsize Park, who she met at a business meeting out there. They married at Burgh House in Hampstead and now have a beautiful daughter called Lila and a son called Oliver.

Joshua is serious about pursuing his music career and is looking to California, where he will also enjoy a good Christian life and where he believes his 'wife to be' is waiting for him. Charlotte and her partner Sunanda are looking towards the East Coast of the USA to immerse themselves in 'Siddha Yoga' which was also my path for many years.

Otherwise life has trundled on, with good times somewhat relieving the worry and anxiety of nursing Joshua through his debilitating toxic illness, which has lasted for years. We are optimistic that this will come to an end and hopefully soon.

This all leaves me here in this overlarge house with the occasional tenant and with my trusted, faithful students who arrive 'on time' each week for their lesson, with some having attended for as long as 25 years.

I really love being a close and regular member of St. Anne's church in Highgate West Hill and surprisingly, the whole routine of early rising on a Sunday morning and then walking a green and scenic route over the heath to the 'Eucharist' service. This also reminds me of my childhood all the way from a village on the windy North East Coast of Yorkshire and the ancient looking church I attended up there.

From here and with whom has yet to be discovered but as always I like new times and new ideas, although as I get older ......maybe not as many challenges!'

Many thanks to Joshua Ben Levy for his added stories and editing, and many thanks to Malcolm Holmes, Tessa Nicolson, Nicholas and Sara Wood and Charlotte Anne Levy for their help.

Lightning Source UK Ltd.
Milton Keynes UK
178481UK00001B/52/P